Freedom and the Public

Public and Private Morality in America

Freedom and the Public

Public and Private Morality in America

DONALD MEIKLEJOHN

SYRACUSE UNIVERSITY PRESS

*Manufactured in the
United States of America*

To
HELEN AND ALEXANDER
MEIKLEJOHN

Preface

These chapters are a development of three lectures delivered in March, 1960, on a grant from the Falk Foundation at the Carnegie Institute of Technology. The lectures originally were enititled "The American Public and Private Interests: Forms of Self-Government." I have been much encouraged by the kindness and sympathetic counsel of Dean Glen U. Cleeton of Carnegie Institute of Technology as I have worked over the original statement to prepare it for publication.

My colleagues and students at the College of the University of Chicago, and at Syracuse University, have provided continuing instruction in the enterprise of formulating philosophic conceptions in the setting of public policy problems. I thank them for that instruction, being assured that they will understand my responsibility for whatever is confused or perverse in the exposition.

DONALD MEIKLEJOHN

Syracuse, New York
April, 1965

Contents

Preface   vii

I. The American Public and Private Interests   1

II. Popular Government—The People Constituted   19

III. Active Government—The People's Business
and the People's Schools   65

IV. Responsible Government—The Freedom of
Public Discussion   101

V. American Freedom and the Wider World   131

Notes to Chapters   155

Index of Names and Cases   161

Freedom and the Public

*Public and Private Morality
in America*

The American Public and Private Interests

AMONG the moral values to which Americans profess allegiance freedom is central. By our devotion to freedom, we say, we distinguish ourselves from our principal opponents in the grand contention of national societies. Yet the freedom we proclaim is, as many Americans conceive it, not a public thing at all. It is rather thought to be a quality of private activities, conducted by individuals and groups. Freedom is won, or held, independently of the American public and its government. Paradoxically, that freedom which we hail as our national blessing is achieved as we attend, not to the nation, but to ourselves.

On the other hand, the American public, of which we are no doubt justly proud, becomes mysterious and elusive as we try to grasp and analyze it. Most Americans, if challenged to assess with candor the goods of public life and private life, will assert that the private goods are primary, if indeed they are not the only goods there are. American individualism issues in the view that the public is hardly real, and certainly best conceived as derivative from private people, private concerns. "It is not America who is so great, or to be great," Whitman wrote, "It is I who am great, it is you, up there . . . and anyone. . . . Underneath all, individuals."[1] Though we celebrate our national achievements with sincerity and confidence, there is much in our thinking which works against the idea that a nation is something which one can be proud of, or celebrate. A nation which is great because of the freedom in it may be, it seems, a mere collection, the loosest of associations. It is not America who is free—only individual Americans.

Our reservations about the public reflect many factors. Intellectually, we find it hard to recognize as real such a whole as a public, in distinction from its elements. Like John Stuart Mill, we find it plausible to explain everything social in terms of the feelings and actions of individuals: we shy at conceding the empirical validity of assertions about collective behaviors, purposes, or responsibilities. In our antimetaphysical fervor we reject common habits of speech in which such collective realities seem assumed; we are not sure that such a thing as a public ever can be "experienced."

On the practical level, too, enthusiasm over collective goods has been discouraged as appearing to endorse the oppressive policies of governments we dislike. European tyrannies have provided ample reinforcement for the antipolitical strains in American thinking. The voice of individual protest has seemed the only salvation from the wasteland of the total state; men assembled are men on the way to corruption. Emerson's ghost stirs at the name of an association; Thoreau finds another tax not to pay; John Brown rides once more to challenge the enslaving customs. It was not only slaves who would be fugitives, it was all Americans—so says the far-gone individualist, who hoped in the new country to escape the political principles which legitimated interference in men's private affairs. Truly, according to this partial but vigorous strain in American thought, to be free is to ignore the public. Private advantage and public welfare are conceived as inherently at odds.

To delineate this paradox is not to contend that the foundations of the Republic are crumbling or that we are committed to perennial self-contradiction. My concern is more modest—it is to locate, and to reduce, a serious confusion in our thinking about politics. Our national soundness no doubt rests on much besides intellectual clarity. And we do, of course, maintain substantial consistency of intention, while sustaining without serious hardship a normal burden of internal stress. We often do better than we think. And yet, we live by our intentions, probably rather more than do other, more custombound, societies.

My thesis is that present American thinking about the public has been confused and sometimes blocked by a lack of clarity about our public and private interests and the moralities in which we try to organize those interests. In the reflections in which we resolve our social conflicts, we have tended to regard such interests as inherently opposed to one another. A good life generally has been conceived as one in which a man pursues his private—that is to say, his own—interests as much as he can, limiting and qualifying this pursuit as he must in the light of public demands. Even when a new President stirs our spirits by urging us to "do for our country," he maintains the separation between self and public; Mr. Kennedy's inaugural did not urge that we simply act as Americans. Our discourse follows the economic model, in which the private interest literally is a man's profit and the public interest appears as reduction of that profit by taxes and other social restraints. To private gain, public advantage appears alien and hostile.

From the opposition between private and public interests it is a short step to identifying freedom with the private sector. There is dependable political potency in the argument that increase in public activity means decrease in freedom. We respond to Mill's contentions that even in a democratic government some men rule the rest and that the purposes which move the rulers can hardly in the end be other than private purposes, identical in quality with those of the ruled. Freedom is, after all, we say, doing what one wants and not what someone else wants. We sometimes concede in theory that freedom may be found in fulfilment of wider intentions. But such intentions always are suspect, always thought liable to assimilation to those "real intentions" to which totalitarians appeal when they tell us that constraint is "true freedom."

Such is our everyday antithesis between freedom and the public; such our persisting paradox in political theory. We cannot live by it. Our positive enthusiasm for freedom certifies our unwillingness to confine our positive values to our private lives. The liberty we proclaim to a sceptical world is more than the absence of restraints upon private activities. Freedom is too important to be left to private individuals.

We can clarify and in a measure resolve this paradox as we study present policy debates about our government and its relation to our business, our schools, and our public discussion.

We can move toward clarity and toward resolution as we bring to bear upon those debates the most enduring themes in American political thinking. For those themes included, especially in the early decades of our national career, that association of freedom with public concerns which I shall assert and defend. Our tradition has not been simple and fully clear, and the division between private and public interests can itself claim a pedigree in our most revered authorities. Yet substantially the lesson which the Founders taught was that the fully free life for Americans requires and is composite of participation in the affairs of the nation they so consciously labored to establish.

An author normally thinks with special interest of the readers who will be disposed, in the first instance, to disagree with him—those whose minds he may hope not only to confirm in the right doctrine they share with him but also to bring from darkness into the light. The present attempt at such intellectual "improving" is made especially arduous by its undertaking to persuade Americans that they have read their own traditions imperfectly. I am proposing, that is, to urge the claims of the public on persons who, themselves members of the public, can in a real sense make my argument false or true by their own positions on the questions here considered. This difficulty is not in principle insuperable, but it presents special problems in all serious discussions of political theory in a self-governing society.

THE COMPLEX HERITAGE OF THOMAS JEFFERSON

Our tradition of freedom as a quality of public activity was well founded in the careers—active and intellectual—of Jefferson and Madison. These men, it seems clear, thought of the national enterprise as a proper domain of human liberty; they hoped that its institutions might afford, in Jefferson's striking phrase, a "substantiation" of freedom. Their conduct and their writings give ample support for the view that on the public stage there may be found those qualities of mind and spirit which attend genuinely free activity. The Virginians did not, as they expended their best energies in the politics of the new nation, conceive themselves committed to a secondary and shadowy enterprise.

And yet in 1775, in a letter to his Tory friend John Randolph (by then fled to England), Jefferson struck the note toward public life which was to become widely characteristic of American attitudes:

> I hope the returning wisdom of Great Britain will, ere long, put an end to this unnatural contest. There may be people to whose tempers and dispositions contention is pleasing, and who, therefore, wish a continuance of confusion, but to me it is of all states but one, the most horrid. My first wish is a restoration of our just rights; my second, a return to the happy period when, consistently with duty, I may withdraw myself totally from the public stage, and pass the rest of my days in domestic ease and tranquillity, banishing every desire of ever hearing what passes in the world.[2]

Jefferson already was a public figure of consequence. Yet he wrote of public business as necessitous, a mere response to duty, to the demands of justice. The self-government to which his subtle and energetic mind seemed committed was a local affair on his own beloved little mountain. There he might indulge his curiosity about nature, his talent in mechanical invention, his devotion to education.

One may speculate how far Jefferson's disclaimers of political interest reflected either a haughty diffidence or a restless conscience. Perhaps he wrote as he did of the wider world of affairs because he already possessed, on his own plantation, that ordered polis which afforded scope for his political talents. Jefferson was a complex man, and his complexity has persisted in the country he helped to fashion. He was notably successful as a constructive statesman—especially, in his own estimation, in his educational program for Virginia. Yet we find him fearing "energetic government" as "nearly always oppressive." We find him declaring in effect that one's own private affairs always are the most interesting, that other men are to be watched with caution, especially when they propose to do good. In Jefferson's writings power appears consistently as prone to corruption rather than useful to public achievement. Ideally, it seems, he would have had each man enjoy his own Monticello, his own concerns, his own aloof perspective on the world below. Such a life would be good in its absorption in family, in friends, the near, the local, the spontaneously social—in a word, in private interests.

It is no superficial piety to attribute to Jefferson's full career a tolerably harmonious synthesis of public and private values resting upon his enduring aspiration for freedom. His active career, construed to frame and balance his writings, manifests this synthesis. But certainly many of his writings, like the letter to Randolph, have given support to those who regard public activity as merely disagreeable necessities. To such, the private life is what "really counts," the only proper area of American freedom. If few say this loudly, many believe it and act in terms of it. And on the other hand, when the indignant patriotic reaction is voiced, those who proclaim the validity of the public's claims assume the same externality of relation between public and private goods. In the hands of self-important patriots today the public is shredded to oaths of allegiance and flag salutes. Between Jefferson public and Jefferson private, between moralistic patriot and self-sufficient private citizen, between Cleon leading the crowd and Socrates against the wall, there is little understanding.

Jefferson's complexity is reflected in his prominence in the rhetoric of both liberal and conservative schools of current political theory. Liberals have stressed the individualistic elements in their argument that private purposes are primary. Conservatives officially contend for the primacy of the community, but only in terms which distinguish this sharply from the "merely convenient" activity of governing. Neither school recognizes intrinsic value in "politics"—the organized life of the public; both regard that life as negative and coercive, a land belonging to no man, occupied transiently by our worser or weaker or less interesting selves. To live well as an American is to live nonpolitically, whether one's guide be one's own wishes or a sanction from on high.

The practical import of these partial readings of Jefferson

has been disastrous. Officially we maintain a decorous devotion to Jefferson's example of public service—our every day is a sort of continuing Fourth of July. But we can spread our patriotism so widely only because it is so thin. We observe the proprieties—we hold our politics to ethical account, but only as barely tolerable instruments of our private intentions. We view with reluctance the commitment of our best talents to government service. In tragically major proportions, we have ruled genuine self-government off the public stage. Men may act there, and carry out public purposes, but their hearts are elsewhere—not because they are bad men but because they are good. Our deepest wish for government is that it "wither away."

Public Freedom as American Tradition

The urgent need of American political morality is to recapture the spirit of that tradition which Jefferson and the other Founders helped to inaugurate. In that tradition, self-government is central. Our intellectual problem is to dig beneath the layers of ceremonial commemoration and sceptical doubt to our effective political commitment, to focus upon the grandeur of our tradition at its center. Our American undertaking was at its early best a striking success in linking men's private and public lives in a morally continuous effort. As we founded the Republic, we did make it possible for an American to maintain his moral propriety as he descended from his Monticello to the political forum.

Our traditions do in fact consecrate freedom as a real quality of a real public. But traditions are not, especially for American intellectuals, genuine working principles. They tend to be political pieties, opiates of the voters, the uniforms that barely cloak our essential diversities. We take our traditions as latecomers, artifices plastered over European usages of long standing. We suspect that taking such pieties too seriously invites disillusionment. That in turn generates a reaction into hyperpiety. The disillusioned and the reactionary schools constitute between them a major component of present-day political theorizing.

The position which I shall try to define and defend here is,

I believe, a viable middle position between these extremes. That self-government which expressed the Enlightenment of the Founding Fathers seems to me still suitable, when purged of scepticism and illusion, to constitute our guiding political morality. We can avoid both despair and reaction by a discriminating return to the essence of political freedom. We can understand and practice that freedom in our public life.

We can, if we will, restore that easy and natural association of morals with politics which once was assumed in American life but which has become largely rhetorical. We can reverse the trend in which freedom has been, effectively, moved outside politics. We can dispute the thesis, held by both the amoral and the moralistic views, that freedom really is something about which politics has nothing to say. We can render plausible the conception of freedom as a society's self-government, as direction by those elements best qualified to direct it.

Such an argument for a proper association in theory of morality with the political order is not an argument for a "total" morality. Neither morality nor politics is all of life, of either private or public life. There are private goods which men pursue in home or garden; and men submit to coercion, indeed, in much of their political behavior. There are broad ranges of public and private activity in which moral criteria are relevant at most only indirectly. In such areas we understand that the goods men seek may well be in opposition to one another; here, fairly enough, adjustment and compromise are appropriate.

The freedom which is properly affirmed of the public, both as a quality of the public's action, and as constitutive of the public, is modest and familiar. It is less imposing than that comprehensively defined freedom which embodies all the intentions, express or implicit, of the entire community. It is less modest than the freedom which is conceived as the simple expression of individual preference—of doing what one wishes without hindrance from man or nature. The overcomprehensive view sanctifies undue interference with individuals in the name of freedom; the overmodest view excludes freedom from important phases of human activity. In fact, freedom is a predicate of some social activity, but also of some individual actions too. Societies can be free, as can individuals, insofar as they are self-governing, which means insofar as they follow principles they impose upon themselves. Society's freedom, so conceived, supports individual freedom in the positive role it provides for individuals in social endeavor. Democratic self-government need not be simply the rule of some men by others. Rulers can be agents, commissioned by the ruled. The terms of the commission are crucial, "terms" signifying both content and limits of the commission. One of the present schools has stressed the positive side of the commission, the other the negative side—but both must be present if the commission is to be fully intelligible.

To the American who asks, "Can I win freedom if I go into politics?" we may thus offer assurances that are public as well as private in import. It is not the case that the widest freedom he may find is that of serving his own personal ambition. It is not the case that as he wins such freedom he must reduce, *pro tanto*, the freedom his fellows may enjoy. It is not the case that entry into politics means descent from the realm of true virtue into a second-class terrain of compromise. It is the case, rather, that there can be won in the political life that advancement of community in which free action by one enlarges the freedom of the rest.

The Resolutions of a Critical Idealism

Resolution of the paradoxes bequeathed by Jefferson to our present-day political thinking is furthered by turning back to the wider context of the eighteenth-century Enlightenment in which Jefferson's thought developed. In Rousseau and Kant, I believe, we find clarifications of self-government rather more useful than the efforts of the utilitarians and the pragmatists. The great Enlightenment idealists were, certainly, committed to the continuity of morals and politics; they believed that the rational self-government which constitutes individual freedom is of one kind with that which makes possible a free society. If not through direct influence on Jefferson or other American thinkers of the Founding period, still in their general impact

on Continental political discussion these men provided fundamental lessons in our understanding of political freedom. They
pointed the way to the rational articulation of idealism and
criticism.

A familiar objection to those lessons is that they assumed
to an excess the reasonableness of men. This objection is quite
unfounded. Rousseau, explaining why he wrote *The Social
Contract* instead of entering actively into politics, replied tartly
that he knew the difference between writing and ruling. When
Kant declared in *Eternal Peace* that it was proper for him to
treat so grand a subject, he observed, with ironic reference to
the graveyard undertones of the subject, that princes need
not be bothered by the thoughts of philosophers. The two men,
so alike and so different, exhibited that mingling of hope and
despair which has consistently informed America's own view
of herself. Like us they learned in their Enlightenment that
the vision of a brighter human future always is attended by
unhappy contrast with the weary and warring society in which
men live.

An American who writes today about self-government cannot speak with the detachment of Rousseau and Kant. He
cannot pretend not to be a citizen-legislator. He cannot be resigned to having his statement of principles brushed aside as
lightly as—on Kant's account—the philosophers were dis-
missed by the Prussian monarchy. The irony, the pessimism,
of a modern American may be all the deeper just because of
our national effort to install every American in the role of
principled participant in the governing process. We have undertaken to constitute a truly self-governing society, and our
difficulties are all too apparent.

I shall try here to follow Rousseau and Kant in the middle
path between the overhopeful and overgloomy views of men
and their politics. The task was formulated, indeed, when
Socrates proposed to defend a clarified Athenian moral and
political faith against both conventional moralists and Sophis-
tic sceptics. The task was effectively carried out, I believe, in
Kant's demonstration of the validity of rational knowledge in
morals and politics as well as in science, with appropriate def-

erence to empirical claims. Kant was right, I am sure, in seeking to establish universality by restricting his purely ethical conception to a "formal" statement. It is in human dignity and the "kingdom of ends" that the Kantian instruction helps us to moderate the modern Leibnizes and to comfort the modern Humes. And it is in these conceptions that we have the intellectual instruments with which to interpret most effectively Jefferson's and Madison's full contributions to American thought. These men were cautious about "abstract ideas" just as Kant was critical of "pure reason." But the Founders were in their political lives committed to that idealist tradition in which moral security is won by effective continuity between private fulfilment and public service.

Can Virtue Be Taught in America?

Emphasis upon our traditions is properly to be balanced by consideration of the ever-renewed ingredient of the new young Americans; and the problem of freedom and the public takes on special urgency when viewed in terms of that education which inducts these new Americans into the adult society. What virtue shall our teachers teach—the development and assertion of these new powers, or the recognition of powers already established? Are the teachers simply to teach the virtue demanded by those who "pay" for the education? How is their teaching to reconcile private innovation with public reverence?

The teacher stands, in relation to the community, where the Founding Fathers stood; indeed it was dominantly as teachers that our idealistic Founding Fathers wrote.[3] They proposed to formulate the basic terms which all later American teachers must convey to those in political authority. They understood that ultimately such authority must render account to those persons—parents or peers or teachers—whose intentions inform the efforts of the formally identified holders of political power. The Fathers knew that the way to instruct rulers is to instruct their advisers. And the basic lesson they left for our teachers is that they must, primarily, make clear the public office and destiny of those whom they teach.

Yet every teacher, whether paid from public or private funds, acknowledges direct and urgent obligations to his pupils, as individual persons. And so the teacher must today as always ask whether he can do full justice to both the new and the old, to both the student and the tradition. He runs the risk of being disloyal to students or adults or perhaps to both if he responds—as he must—to the special demands of his own academic brotherhood.

An American teacher today need not fall into one or another of these disloyalties. Teachers often achieve, perhaps uniquely in America, that substantial freedom which is one with the freedom of other persons in the community. But our teaching practice, especially in dealing with society, shows wide confusion about how private and public interests should be related in our teaching. Our instruction in politics vacillates between doctrinaire exhortation and weary realism. We tend to explain our economy as the scene of unrelieved private interest, with occasional reminders of the blessings of generosity. Our schools themselves have been conceived as preparing young people either for private gaining or private spending. Our cherished forum of public discussion is viewed as an arena of private assertions, no one of which is particularly responsive to any other. Friendly though we are as domestic creatures, we are too innocent to think of people of other countries except as strangers.

The symptom of our confusion in education is its dominantly moralistic tone. True to the dichotomy between public and private interests, we phrase our problem quantitatively, asking how much a teacher, or a student, may reserve to his private affairs, how much he must delegate to the public. A teacher is supposed to exhort the future citizens with respect to their public duties. But if he is candid with his students, he also has explained what private advantages also are attainable. Public and private claims can be at best compromised. The level rarely is reached where public and individual career interests are continuous. It is merely quaint, or boring, to apply to a college Woodrow Wilson's motto for the Princeton of 1896—"in the Nation's service."

A college or university teacher can escape such confusion, can undertake the delicate task of "character-building," whether of private or of public person, only if he contrives to stand between public and pupil with full candor toward both. His task is precisely to promote an intellectual, as well as a simply moral, treatment of the relation between public and private interests. He must be able to advance the diffusion of such knowledge as will show those interests to be continuous. How far such knowledge is possible he can not be certain. But he teaches on the premise that to understand the nature and range of public and private interests is to reduce the tension between them and make the cultivation of each more significant. The self-examined lives of public person and private person may be discovered to be committed to the same objectives.

It is thus inherent in the present undertaking that light be thrown on the kind of knowledge we need to educate for public and private purposes. The term "knowledge" is not very satisfactory, especially if it is employed so as to exclude "wisdom" or "intelligence." The more instructive phrase probably is "common knowledge," referring to both the quality and the diffusion of the mental condition. "The public wills the good it does not see," Rousseau said; our problem is to help the public develop the intellectual acumen of the man who "sees the good he does not will." Whatever our term, it is generality of thought that is crucial. The prime need of the American public is to know and discriminate among general principles, to define formally its relation to private persons.

The Problems of John Dewey

The argument here retraces in part the course of John Dewey's 1926 lectures, *The Public and Its Problems*. Dewey saw the public's problems as intellectual, not so much in seeking means to given ends as in calling for deliberation on competing ends, or on competing programs for action. The public's problems were intellectual in requiring self-discovery in identifying and clarifying one's own purposes. Dewey, like Socrates and Freud, focused his attention on the therapy of self-awareness, of locating and analyzing amorphous irritations so that one can know what and where they are and can manage them. Only with such knowledge could the public be said to exist.

It was characteristic of Dewey that he played down the theme of the private challenge to public authority. Americans have divided their world, he observed, into private and public affairs and see the two in a state of constant tension. This tension Dewey sought to relax by stating it as intellectual. He insisted on the reality of groups as well as of "biological individuals"; he argued that the grand antithesis between individual and society is misleading. Each has its own integrity to establish, its own knowledge to develop. The achievement of the Great Community would bring about that continuous social knowledge in which public and private concerns would assume right relations. Tensions of will would not all disappear, but they would be, as Dewey hoped, rendered amenable to thoughtful deliberation.

Dewey's argument offered a fair challenge to the America of the 1920's and also of the 1950's when the book was republished. Yet its impact is hardly all that Dewey hoped for. The public has not advanced far toward conceiving its problems as intellectual. They still are conceived in terms of will rather than understanding, as involving the submission, as necessary, of a private good to a public interest external to it. The public's interests are taken to be a maximum pile of private interests; the public as such is not thought to seek a good itself. Among the theorists, the "pluralists" who owe much to Dewey conceive the desirable polity, in a fashion attributed to Federalist Paper Ten, as an equilibrium of clashing interests, no one of which should be too strong. On the other side, exponents of a new, or very old, natural right have denounced Dewey and have asserted ever more urgently the distinction between an intrinsic private good and a public welfare that is a shadowy compound of prudence and necessity. In our affirmations of economic and academic freedom alike we announce the individual's business as "his own" and beyond the reach of legitimate government. And in our civil liberties efforts we again pose that opposition of individual to society which John Stuart Mill proclaimed and which Dewey tried vainly to banish from public discussion. To the individual's question why he should concede to the public, the only relevant answer is, "You'd better."

It is no summary refutation of John Dewey that his therapy did not noticeably improve his patient. It does seem that the very diagnosis which Dewey offered of the Great Society's troubles implied that the arrival of the Great Community might not be imminent. Dewey's account of America's development, in which the effective internal dynamic was contrasted with merely epiphenomenal ideas thrown off like sparks in the process, suggested that the ideas would be unlikely to regulate or even illuminate the development. Since he delivered the lectures, the depression and the Second World War and now the fear of a third war have provided no very favorable context for clear thinking about the public. It is not simply Dewey's New England self-distrust that makes us nod our heads at the unresponsiveness of Americans to his prescriptions. One who insists that revolutionary ideas follow revolutions rather than precede them can hardly be surprised if, in the time of the shaking of nations, the scope of social change is not at once reflected in a comparable revolution of thought about the public and its problems.

Yet if, assuming as well as we can John Dewey's patience and persistence, we try to understand why his prescription was not more fully followed, we are led to challenge some of the ingredients of that prescription. In general, Dewey's deficiency seems to lie not in his affirmative analysis but in his negations. On the positive side there comes through his sober prose the sense of life richly and strenuously lived. Some of his denials too seem well founded, such as his rejection of the Hegelian metaphysical state and of the allegedly rigid individualism in the natural rights theory. But Dewey's rejections went further, to insist upon a transiency and secondary status to general ideas. He was reluctant to countenance admission of that kind of permanence, or indeed eternity, which might provide a frame and a coherence for the persisting flux

of experience. Quite literally, we may say that Dewey had
difficulty in persuading Americans to change their thinking
because he had himself trouble in adequately conceiving
change or making it intelligible. In his pragmatic philosophy
change tends to be barely succession. In his account there is
lacking that "mental" operation of holding new and old together which is necessary if they are to be elements in a single
policy or program.

Whether this criticism is fair to Dewey, or instructive for
us, depends on how it can be elaborated with respect to particular problems, on whether we can so understand the changing aspects of self-government as to identify elements of permanence as well as of novelty. I believe that only in this way
can we advance that progress in community which Dewey
regarded as the heart of the democratic enterprise. To know
ourselves fully, as a public, is to know our enduring purposes,
to know ourselves kinsmen of the dead as well as of the un-
born. Such knowledge is both essential to the existence of a
public and consistent with the experimental principles which
Dewey insistently proclaimed.

I propose, then, to take issue with Dewey's assertion of the
obsolescence of all social and political principles. *The Public
and Its Problems* contends that the political ideals of the
eighteenth century are not fitting for the twentieth century. In
a sense—somewhat abstract—this is true; but in another and
more fundamental sense it is false. The Founding Fathers, in
their effective doctrine, do provide a plausible starting point
for American political theory. If, heeding their own advice, we
change some of our ideas with each generation, we must be
able to explain the change in the light of what went before.
It is no accident that in the realm of ideas only that reform
which is continuous with the past has much hope of success.

The Present Perplexities of the Public

To claim that despite the efforts of John Dewey the public
still has generic problems is to say that there persists in some
measure that eclipse of the public which Dewey took as his
central problem. Notwithstanding our tremendous machinery

for maintaining our body politic, we lack a really clear understanding of what this public is, of what *a* public is, and of
how it is related to private interests. And a public which does
not know itself cannot educate.

American life in the latter half of the twentieth century is
dominated by affluence on the one hand and cold war tension
on the other. Neither is conducive to serious thought about
our common affairs. Our prosperity diverts us by both its
charms and its uncertainty. Our hostility to the Communists
moves us to mobilize our defenses rather than our reflections
about what we want to defend. The public activated by such
threats is cloudy and inferior. It locates common interests in
superficial and unelevating concerns. It promises to yield, like
its antecedent of 1918, to a "normal" concentration on private
affairs. Our problem, in the days of the New Frontier, is how
to combine the alertness requisite to defense with the reflective community of the secure settlement. We have to find how
to define a genuine public morality on a basis more than military—how to be wise and also brave enough to be free.

Much is made of the present need for leadership. But we
impose on our leaders in all fields an incoherent responsibility
toward those whom they lead. The political candidate has to
try to move his constituents—by appeals to their private aspirations—toward some public good. The official of a voluntary association must serve his own partial public without
parochial commitment against the wider society. The intellectual leader must contrive to refine the tastes of others without appearing simply to impose his own preferences. The
business leader must make money for his stockholders while
observing a due concern for consumers, labor, and the rest of
society. The teacher, most of all, must somehow bring into
effective adaptation the maturing power of his students to a
world they never made. All these leaders have to speak for
a public of whose character and concerns no one is well informed.

Neither our material wealth nor our military posture is today congenial to inducting our young people into a realm of
expanding freedom. Our economy offers progressively less

chance for the "man on the make." The public education of
the young is first of all an induction into the liabilities of
military service, or at least into the hazards of the semimilitary
situation. Small wonder if, in the face of these, the serious
lesson we teach is noncommittal submission. Small wonder if
obligations to the public appear as matters to be discharged
rather than deliberated. Small wonder that college students
resort to existentialist demonstrations and confrontations.

These chapters intend, then, to present freedom as a public
good, to assert—with due respect to the Founders and to
present theorists—freedom as a quality of public activity. The
argument will seek to show that there is a public, a real public,
definably related to the persons and groups which make it up,
and that this public can achieve freedom insofar as what it
does issues from properly ordered relations between it and its
constituents.

To explain these properly ordered relations requires consideration of three distinct but closely interrelated themes,
which are taken up in the next three chapters. There is first
the generic theme of popular self-government; our inquiry
here is how far the prevailing unpopularity of government can
be overcome—how far government can be seen as the full expression of common interests, how far, indeed, it serves to
bring the public into being. Secondly, assuming that a known
and knowing government can be a popular government, we
ask about how it must govern in the fields of our economic
and educational affairs. And thirdly, we look behind, or above,
government to consider its right relation to those processes of
public discussion which, given a known and active government,
maintain its responsiveness to the public will. To know and
be known, to be active, and to respond to publicly discussed
principles are the essentials of the freedom the American public must enjoy. And it must enjoy these, not only in its own
affairs, but also, as the final chapter will try to explain, as it
faces dramatically urgent responsibilities in a world where
political freedom still is an uneasy newcomer.

Popular Government—The People Constituted

AMERICANS are taught to believe in self-government. But everywhere they are warned against the government they have set up. They are saluted as sovereign voters; yet they are tendered commiserations appropriate to men oppressed. They are told that their government will make them free and also that it will enslave them.

We live, truly, with Rousseau's paradox. And if the statement of that excited Frenchman was not fully clear, we have doubtless muddled it further with insistent admixtures of Anglo-Saxon prudence. We must have self-government—of that our traditions have made us certain. We must have a public agency that is of us, responsive to our deep, as to our transient, desires. But such an agency is costly and intellectually strenuous and dangerous to our private independence. And so throughout our national career we have fenced our public activities in to reduce the cost and keep life simple and above all leave us free for our private business. The American public has been a shadowy and elusive thing, a flitting paternal ghost on the battlements of the busied castle which is our American home.

We speak of our government as resting on the governed's consent. But the meaning we attach to consent is dominantly negative. It is tolerant rather than eager. We do not, as free men, achieve full spontaneity and enrichment in our organized relations with our fellows. We do not make our government popular as embodying our concerted will. We are not willing, in the governing process, to undertake to broaden and refine our common interests. Consent we may, but only because we must.

We are aware that a merely negative stance is inadequate to

19

our political mission. Adherents of the contract theory of government always have been taunted to produce the papers that show the literal pledge of allegiance, to account for the cases in which a citizen is less than fully in accord with his government. In reply the theory has invoked as a rule some reference to a consent that is silent. But this is persuasive only as the silence is filled by common activities actually undertaken. The problem of American self-government may be summed up, essentially, in the difficulty we have in discovering occasions, other than military functions and patriotic celebrations, on which we are able to act as Americans together. We have feared that concerted action will be contaminated by any association with "politics."

The early American tradition of government as positive in moral import confronts today a new folklore, claiming a basis in hard experience, in which response to government is negative and grudging. How to reconcile the conflict, how to resolve it in favor of the government genuinely popular, is, I believe, our most urgent need in political theory. We must show our politics as the energizing center of our effective morality, the realm, not of selfless service by some to others, but of activating and quickening our common interests.

We must, in other words, achieve such understanding of our public business as makes it more than a series of unwelcome intrusions into our private concerns. Such understanding requires, as Dewey suggested, an earnest reinstatement of empirical methods in studying politics; it involves the recognition that private undertakings are not alone to be associated with spontaneity nor public with coercion. Such understanding further requires a willingness—on which Dewey often frowned—to direct and clarify such observations by the moral conceptions which form the heart of self-government. We have to show that such direction can be consistent with the most rigorous responsiveness to "fact," and that lacking such direction both observations and policies are aimless.

We need, in other words, to achieve that freshness of perspective which is the ideal of the contemporary "realist" school of political theory, but we need to understand as well that mere fidelity to facts is an empty triumph. What facts? The realist replies, "true behaviors, as distinct from traditional folklores"; but the realist makes his own selections in terms of his own judgments of relevance. In political study, it seems clear, the critique of traditional ends and methods must be paralleled by the assurance of continuity with those ends and methods. Without such continuity we are left with Dewey's dilemma—that if all our political ideals are just "war-cries," it is unreasonable to ask that one be regarded as more suitable than another.

We need to pursue, on the level of political theory, the question of how the great ideal of genuinely popular government may be realized under present-day conditions. We need to avoid being misled by flag-waiving folklore, but we need equally to avoid being taken in by more sophisticated folklores. We have constantly to distinguish between what people say and what they truly believe.

We need, once again, to make it clear to the freedom-seeking American that government is his friend, indeed his fellow, in the search for fuller and more significant freedom. It is absurd that Americans should consign a major part of their associated activities to a moral slum, where good men fear to tread and absentee landlords profit from the misbehavior of reluctant residents. On the other hand, it is only in the effective extension of our common morality to all of our community that we attain that full freedom which is responsiveness to principles we all share.

Are there, in fact, moral predicates that can be affirmed of the United States as a national community? Can the United States be judged as a moral agent—as brave or generous or prudent or wise or self-restrained? Can it be judged refined in its tastes? A simple yes or no answer to any of these is hard to make plausible. One school of thought, claiming, perhaps, lineage from Plato, holds that the social personality manifests all the traits characteristic, on a small scale, of individuals. Another school insists that such predication is metaphorical; though, as Hume's example suggests, explanation in terms of metaphor may be hard to stop short of absurdity. It is sufficient to assert some moral predicates of the body politic —predicates such as honesty and justice. And with these there must go such ascription of freedom and responsibility as inheres in moral character in general.

To say that the nation can exhibit moral character or its lack is meaningful only if the government is understood to formulate and express the nation's moral intentions. We cannot say that the United States is good because its people are good though its government is bad. Government is what the people employ as the vehicle of their common aim. Insofar as it is bad so are they as well. The business of government, so far as it is genuinely representative, is to catch and convey the people's spirit in its dealings, either with its own citizens or with other nations.

All this is indeed ritually familiar to every school child as the heart of our national tradition. It is the smiling mask at the patriotic celebration, the political convention. Our problem is to see and understand it as also the true expression of America's political intentions. We have to appreciate our government as qualified to develop and bring to actuality the fullness of what we wish our common life to be.

THE FOLKLORE OF AMERICAN GOVERNMENT[1]

Beside the official political traditions in the United States and often overshadowing them there has evolved a folklore or mythology in which our government is hardly to be conceived as making for the good life. Some of the governors may so regard it, but most who work for government think of it as just their job. The governed tolerate their government but rarely cheer it. We are shy about committing too many first-class energies to the work of governing. In part, this is because we still believe, with Mill, that ability in government must be balanced by ability outside. But it is more because our private affairs are so attractive. If we ask the welfare state to do for us more than the night-watchman state did, we still think of welfare mainly as public charity. Government's role is to assure that Scrooge, having made his pile, share some of it with others less shrewd. Eminence in government is resolved into maximum public giving with minimum public expense.

Even in our provisions against force and fraud we have believed we should not pay our public agents too much. We have imposed a heavy burden on our consciences and our customs to maintain that order in which liberty can be assured. Limited indeed, despite recent progress, is the number of public officials whose talents are certified in the activities which Americans admire. "Our great men," Rossiter quotes a late nineteenth-century American, "cannot afford to take political office, and you and I cannot afford to put them there."[2] An intellectual Presidential candidate rarely is favored by professional politicians; successful liberal candidates for Congress learn the intractability of the establishment once they are in office. We have been reluctant to make too much of the distinction that occasionally has qualified public officials. We have demanded of our leaders a rigorous and unexpansive probity, with a minimum of imagination and a maximum of determination.

We have on occasion asked for "real" leadership. But the leaders we have regarded as congenial with self-government have been hardly more than delegates, persons who would do literally what the people wanted them to do. In emergencies, we have looked for men whose striking energy could inspire courage if rarely reflection. So far as we have thought it important for high officials to possess intellectual quality, we have conceived that quality in a fashion instrumental and secondary. We rarely have asked, or wished, that political leaders should be able to discover our national will to us, to bring our enduring purposes to bear on our situation so that the direction of our common enterprise becomes clear.

The test which we normally apply to candidates for high office is the test of private morality so triumphantly met by Walt Kelly's presidential candidate Fremount, the small insect of the "Pogo" cartoon, whose only known utterance is the cheerful "Jes' fine!" If we must invest men with authority, our first concern is to see that they do not rob or cheat or discourage us. We cannot be hurt by one who, wherever he looks, reports that everything is "Jes' fine!"

A genuinely popular government must be a government of ideas, and the most critical weakness of our government today is the difficulty that ideas have in it. Our current folklore tells us that the more general an idea the more numerous its enemies. The most obvious result has been insistence on a narrow construction of the national purpose, the subjection of all new or expansive programs to a steep uphill route to confirmed popularity. The only recurrent exceptions are in the areas of concerted negation—the areas of war and parsimony and the punishment of disloyalty.

To ask of a government that it become truly popular is to require that government, through each returning day and month and year, carry out that set of purposes which, were the people fully informed and utterly sober of mind, they would identify as the object of their common will. To speak of a "common will" at all is to rouse the suspicions of empirical political thinkers. And it implies an effort indeed prodigious, on the part of both government and people, to find that which all can best agree upon, taking into account the demands of the long run as well as the short, and the need for action as balanced by the need for deliberation. It involves that element of ultimate popular appeal on which Rousseau insisted; with us it also must involve the activity of representatives who can, as Madison thought, formulate public purposes better than citizens at large. This is indeed highly complicated, and empiricists may well be sceptical how far we can ever approach fulfilment of these conditions.

Apart from the feasibility of such responsiveness to a true popular demand, its value also is questioned. To many followers of de Tocqueville, the equality implicit in democracy is necessarily the enemy of excellence. Ideas widely popular can hardly be subtle or refined. Aristocracy's disappearance has, they fear, removed the best obstacles to majority tyranny. A government which wins mass popularity will reflect the people at their worst.

Present discontents normally turn the attention to a mere

cheerful past, and some contemporary writers look back to our early local associations as a model for popular government as well as for bridling popular impulse. There is strong appeal in the image of the small community, where the chances for identity of interests were high and where a voter could judge his agents at close range. The town meeting did, Walter Lippmann noted in *Public Opinion,* establish our dominant political stereotype. The image of the omnicompetent citizen could match the idea of a government which was simple, efficient, often changed, and so responsive to the people's intentions. Yet Lippmann argued that from the first we managed our affairs by ignoring the stereotype. Hamilton was Lippmann's hero, precisely because Hamilton understood that government must be attached to a limited segment of the population if it were to serve the national interest as a whole. To a degree, Lippmann concluded, a government must be unpopular if it is to serve ends which are quite as important as self-government—ends such as peace, comfort, and beauty. We cannot, Lippmann claimed, have complete self-government and also wise government.[3] In fact, the limitations of the self-contained community and the omnicompetent citizen led us to resort to "force, patronage and privilege" to hold our politics together. The New England model faded into folklore, and folklore faded gives way to unadorned "practicality."

THE WORLD WARS AND THE AMERICAN PUBLIC

To speak of many present political ideas as folklore is not to deny either their power or their partial fidelity to their background. Twice in the past half-century we have gathered ourselves in a strenuous national effort and each time have had to deflect that effort into making war. In each of the World Wars we were fortunate to have entered the struggle after a period of national consolidation. But in terms of the quest for an enduring national self-consciousness, these sequences were tragic. Like a young man who must, just as his powers reach full maturity, turn to military routines, the United States, gathering itself under Wilson and later under Franklin Roosevelt, had to focus its collective energies of body and spirit on making war. We can only speculate on what we might otherwise have been; in some ways the wars sustained the national growth, but they hardly worked in the most important sense to forward the sense of effective national community.

Thus in Wilson's first administration the mustering into government of impressive personal talents and the institution of new agencies were submerged in mobilization for war. At the war's end Wilson was unable to carry the country with him in pursuit of a national commitment to international order. Having heightened our energies to win the war we were unable to maintain the temper essential to help assure the peace. Wilson's failure was, it seems, his inability to come to terms with local political realities. He could not command that support which might have been decisive in forestalling the European tragedies of the next twenty years. America was not ready to act with such speed on a matter of such importance.

Ironically, in the period after the First World War, our scepticism over morality in public affairs was reinforced by our supremely negative enterprise in collective moral improvement—Prohibition. No doubt it was easier after our wartime mobilizations of moral force to make war on the evils of drink than to try our patience with the management of international disorder and domestic instability. But the very pathos of the Noble Experiment bore witness to the attenuation of national enthusiasm. Normalcy meant return to inconsequential politics.

With the advent of depression, the New Deal, in uneven fashion, afforded opportunities in government for new and conspicuous energies. If the country did not effect a wholesale revision of its economic and political ideas, it did adopt enough new procedures to upset defenders of the established faith. The New Deal exhibited government, more clearly than for many years, as the bearer of national purpose.

But like the New Freedom, the New Deal was overwhelmed by war before it had the chance, or the uneasy responsibility, of developing a positive program for American life. As Samuel Lubell pointed out in *The Future of American Politics*, the various elements in the New Deal coalition were bound together mainly by the common experience of being underprivileged. Their loyalty to the coalition tended to be limited by the duration of their respective opportunities, as private interest groups, to gain by staying in the coalition. In fact, both major parties were loose combinations of interest groups whose common principles were casual and transitory.

Our concern here is with attitudes toward government, and we must note that the New Dealers, though generally willing to expand government's activity, were not palpably eager to challenge government's popularity in theoretical terms. Wide credence was given to the thesis that our failing after World War I had been to undertake too much in the way of a national crusade. Again, American liberals traditionally have distrusted centralized power. The New Deal was marked by the diversity of overlapping and often conflicting agencies. New Deal spokesmen were occupied, not with defending active government, but rather with breaking down the defenses of established propriety. In the arguments over public policies which reached their sharpest form before the Supreme Court, New Deal spokesmen like Thurman Arnold announced themselves sceptical of the stability of all public policy principles. Their mottoes were John Dewey's: "Up with Change!", "Down with Absolutes!", "All is Folklore and Symbol!" The critics of the conservative Court took their stand, not so much on a thesis about the duties and limits of government as on the desirability of change in general. Whither to change might not be clear, but formal prescriptions should not be in the way. And as long as the country had many millions out of work, any suggestion that we "do something" was plausible. It remained so until the unemployed finally were absorbed into the United States Army in the war years. But its plausibility reflected, too, our inability to try to articulate a serious national program. We shrank from committing to our government a mission of comprehensive popularity.

We might have made progress in that direction had not World War II come upon us. And now, after we have "won the war," denunciation of our enemies still is the dominant note in our political thinking. To avoid being totalitarian requires, it is thought, great caution about all government—

especially a government bearing gifts sugared with common enthusiasm.

THE PRESENT STRAINS OF THEORY: SCEPTICS AND BELIEVERS

The New Deal pragmatism, in its antitotalitarian form, probably still exerts dominant influence on our political theorists; most of its adherents showed no particular uneasiness in their assignment to command posts along the New Frontier.[4] As distilled into theory it is heavily negative in flavor. It does not deny all virtue to political activity, or politicians, but on principle it denies too much of anything to anybody. It is urgent against extremes, rigidities, absolutes. It approves relativities, flexibilities, moderations. It is border state mentality with respect to consciences and peculiar institutions. It is for experiments. It commends men at all levels, from the Supreme Court down, who are strong on self-restraint. It holds that having a theory is of doubtful worth, since the theory may be wrong.

This modern sophistry is not at present unchallenged. There has developed what we may fairly consider a counter Reformation, a school of conservative conviction which proposes that we should apply in politics such substantive standards of right and wrong as are familiar in our private, or as some say, our "social," existence. This position is advanced in differing styles by John Hallowell, Russell Kirk, Clinton Rossiter, and Leo Strauss. It is concerned primarily with morality and with avoiding the debasements of popular taste; it meets the problem of government's unpopularity by conceiving government as "the community's highly developed instrument for compelling justice and order."[5] If courts and legislators and administrators will follow true moral principles, in their conduct and in the purposes they serve, say these authors, we will escape the contrast between moral men and immoral politics. And so these new conservatives issue what we may fairly title the Call to Public Virtue.

On the other side, theorists of the pragmatic view, as they consider where morality may genuinely be found in public affairs, have stressed the wealth and variety of the so-called voluntary associations that spangle the American scene. Of this Reformation, as fully articulated, we may say that "pluralism"[6] is the characteristic slogan—a pluralism that assigns to politics the limited merit of permitting a hundred, or a thousand, flowers of associated activity to bloom as men's spirits or appetites move them. This school's unifying battle cry we may term the Praise of the Private Association.

I shall review each school in some detail and shall try to show that neither gives a satisfactory answer to our questions about freedom and the public. In neither view is there provision for conceiving government as genuinely popular. Each theory suffers from a characteristic excess. The Call to Public Virtue insists that political thought must start with and issue in morality, but it prescribes a substantive creed, supposed to govern public and private affairs alike, which cannot in fact be popular with more than a limited number of people. The liberal view, reacting on behalf of freedom, declines to acknowledge as valid for directing government any morality which is not "freely chosen" by an individual or a private association.

For the Call to Public Virtue, government is an instrument to carry out purposes embodied in a code affirmed by true believers and imposed, willy-nilly, on those as yet unenlightened. For the Praise of the Private Association, government is a traffic policeman, according a mechanically equal chance to each man and group but expressing no independent moral authority of his own. In each view, indeed, government is in some sense an agent. But in neither is government commissioned by the governed to carry out their common interests. For the conservative, government is in a lower world of practical activity which can at best copy the example of the initiated. For the liberal, government is a derivative activity which responds only indirectly to men's serious purposes.

The conservative pins his hopes on the moral public and relegates freedom to a lowly order of being. The liberal exalts freedom, with attendant indifference to the public as a source of moral claims. Each view consequently refuses support to the conception of a government that truly governs and still is popular. The conservative resigns himself to governing that is an imposition of the "uncommon" people upon the common; indeed, in sensitive reaction against imposition he puts his first hopes on example, suggestion, and the assistance of school and church. But in the conservative society, most of the people cannot truly speak of the government as their own. The liberal, per contra, is too eager for spontaneity of persons and groups to grant to government that energy and scope it must have if those persons and groups are to live in harmony and in fulfilment of their most expansive interests. The liberal assumes a pre-established unity to which the common man will naturally attune himself—he is as optimistic as his conservative counterpart is pessimistic about the propensity of persons and groups to live sociably. For the liberal, government is a rather unfortunate and unfriendly surd in a generally amiable social scene.

THE CALL TO PUBLIC VIRTUE

The current Counter Reformation in political theory is diverse. Its multiplicity is intimated by the fact that Rossiter, as he cuts the cloth for the new conservatism, concedes that in America such an effort must borrow from the language of liberalism. And wearers of borrowed clothes often lack uniformity.

The sense of the movement is well conveyed through one of its early historical expressions. The Call—or Command—to Public Virtue was sounded sternly from the steeples of the Massachusetts Puritans. Their central tenets were, as Rossiter describes them, imposing: the depravity of all men and the political incompetence of most; the natural inequality of men and consequent inevitability of orders and classes; government by an ethical aristocracy, chosen from men with a stake both religious and economic in the going order; government which, for the glory of God, the good order of the community, and the salvation of souls, might regulate the lives and enterprises of men to the most minute detail; the existence, in the Scriptures, "of a perfect rule for the direction and government of all men in all duties which they are to perform to God and man"; the consequent necessity that men obey the laws and defend the traditions of a society based on this divine blueprint; the confinement of change and reform to that which can and must take place in the hearts of men; and finally, the preciousness of liberty, but of that liberty, as John Winthrop said, "to that only which is just, good, and honest," a "liberty maintained and exercised in a way of subjection to authority."[7]

Present-day conservative writers display no such united front as prevailed in colonial Massachusetts. If some Puritans preserve their ancient faith, so do some southerners and many diverse spokesmen of the West. There is not available in America as a whole a common creed that might govern a common life "to the most minute detail." There is no obvious basis on which an ethical hierarchy might be established.

Appeal to the lessons of Puritan New England or the antebellum South is hardly more than a gentle exercise in nostalgia. It does provide support for the thesis on which the new conservatives in fact most nearly agree: that Americans once had, but now have lost, a sense of national character and national mission. Like other peoples, they say, we have been diverted by the crowding business of a rewarding material world. We need to be reawakened to fundamental moral principles. The Call is to fundamental Virtue and to that higher law which defines that Virtue. American life has suffered from a surfeit of liberty.

Apart from this negative position, it is hard to find agreement among the new conservatives as to where in our nation's or our culture's past we should look for our standard of fundamental Virtue. Leo Strauss seems to urge a return to Aristotle, to a conception of natural justice with antedates and avoids the "unfortunate" departures into "modern natural right" engineered by Hobbes and Locke.[8] Others like John Hallowell accept seventeenth-century doctrine without express admission of conflict with "classical natural right"; they find in the Declaration of Independence a basis for the ethic that should pervade our public life.[9] Rossiter confines himself in the main to urging "True Conservatives" to deepen their sense of religion's import for politics. It is not surprising that a single ethical basis is hard to formulate. Metaphysics has long since been, among intellectuals, a private affair. And the "minute details" which are to be governed are heterogeneous and controversial—they range over aid to schools, birth control, divorce, liquor, decency, the meaning of a "church establishment," and the "free exercise of religion."

The form of the conservative position most likely in the American context to secure wide support is no doubt that which takes its start from the metaphysics in the Declaration of Independence. This is Hallowell's theme, as he argues that the conceptions of nature's law, and of natural rights, must control our political thinking. In these we have recourse directly to the true nature of Man. Hallowell may point with plausibility to the rhetoric of American protests against mistreatment of minorities: the rights of men, as men, always have appealed to Americans.

The new conservatives are not content to affirm such rights in the "abstract"; they follow the Puritans in asserting that a detailed substantive code is indispensable to a true social philosophy. Hallowell does not limit himself to asserting human dignity or equal protection of law as a sufficient moral prescription for public conduct. This would, he says, repeat the "merely formal" fallacy in older liberalism. Such a prescription cannot "stand alone"—it can be sustained only if conceived as ordained by a higher power.[10] A merely formal concord of wills would, he claims, fail of intellectual conviction: "with the gradual abandonment of the substantive conception of law, when the formal conception of law alone is retained, liberalism becomes degenerate, preparing the way for its own destruction. . . . Cut loose from its moorings in faith reason drifted with the tides of opinion, no longer able to distinguish the true from the false, the good from the bad, the just from the unjust." Only the substantive conception of a higher law, of eternal truths discoverable by reason, could have sustained the individual conscience.

The substantive conception of law carries us beyond respect

for human dignity to such a prescription of particular moral qualities as was set forth by John Winthrop. It is not freedom, primarily, but justice, virtue, order, and excellence that are the social ultimates. These are the public virtues which it is the business of governors, as of good women and preachers and college professors, to promote with zeal. These it is the special task of American schools and colleges to develop; our pupils must become tuned to the Call to Public Virtue before their ears are exposed to more alluring or more deafening cries.

Adherence to such a "substantive" public morality involves the conviction that a society which tries to school its young in proper loyalty must employ more than mere forms or procedures. Abstractions like "formal respect for persons" will not, say the new conservatives, supply the stimulus adequate to resist the various Public Vices abroad in the world. They will not be proof against brainwashing. Americans old and young can be made virtuous only by concrete representations of courage, self-sacrifice, temperance, intellectual refinement, piety, generosity, and other variants of the classic virtues. It is understood that conformity to such standards can never be wholly spontaneous, but it is believed that enthusiastic enforcement will be—even if imposed—more efficient and really more kind than a laggard effort to remain "popular."

Though such virtues, when specified to practice, hardly form a pattern which can fairly be said to be accepted by all Americans, it may be presented by the new conservatives as at least the defining content for our basic common education. If it is hard to say what a public morality can be which should direct government, at least it must govern the proper training of the young. This is perhaps the most appealing element in the Call to Public Virtue. At its best, its tone and emphasis are paternal. As such, it speaks to the parent, or child, that is in each of us. As such, it speaks also to the teacher or pupil in each of us. We are more than willing to acknowledge that in character, as in mind, we have much to learn. The special theme of the Call to Public Virtue is that for adult citizens, as well as for children, society must play the role of parent or parent-teacher. Such is the theme of many sensitive southerners in the United States as they try to define the proper relation of whites to Negroes. Though some American teachers are deeply perplexed over how to educate the capacity to be wisely free, the exponents of the Call profess little perplexity. For them common moral knowledge should guide public as well as private conduct. To disseminate that knowledge is the proper mission of a good government.

Of the forms of public education to which Americans recently have been exposed, none have been more impressive than the opinions of the Supreme Court, and especially in cases involving the interpretation of the First Amendment. The Supreme Court does not, normally, introduce into its reading of the Constitution explicitly "moral" criteria. But according to the new conservatives it should do so. This is the import of the energetic criticism of the Court by Professor Walter Berns in *Freedom, Virtue and the First Amendment*. The Court has erred, he thinks, in not restricting speech to that which is virtuous. The Court has failed—in handling problems of censorship, of incitement to violence, and of Communist associations—to appeal to the criteria of decency, patriotic loyalty, and peacefulness in persuasion. In Berns' argument, decisive importance appears attached to the character of the speaker, who rates low in social value if he is pornographic or unsettling or conspiratorial. In such categories we may find a sufficient delineation of public good, of a universal and substantive standard by which to measure men and policies.

There are, as I have noted, differences among the new conservatives: Berns is at pains to dissociate himself from many tenets held by others in the group as well as from advocacy of a crude imposition of common morality. But in his insistence upon a substantive, as distinct from a formal principle of public good, Berns is at one with Hallowell and Strauss. The "Straussian" collection of essays which attack the "scientific" approach to politics[11] insist upon the superiority of "common moral sense" to that "political science" which inspires or issues in studies of voting or interest groups or administration. Yet this common moral sense turns out to be quite special, something other than the judgment of the man in the street. In his culminating "Epilogue," Strauss sets forth the following criticisms of the "new political science": it is devoted to democracy because it is unable to distinguish between one desire and another; it is "vulgarian" in lacking a sense for what is noble; it is based on a dogmatic atheism; it cannot make out a case for our form of society against communism; it denies that there is a difference between things high and things low and thus denies that men differ from brutes—it contributes to the victory of the gutter; it culminates in observations made by "people who are not intelligent about people who are not intelligent."[12] The scientific students of politics and the great mass of those whom they study are thus excluded from the Virtuous.

THE CALL REJECTED

The Call to Public Virtue has not attracted a great number of Americans. But its devotees exhibit little dismay. They enjoy the positive sense of a crusade in which American—and Eternal—Good is defended against Foreign—and also Eternal —Evil. They are confident, since they speak for man's true nature, that the world is on their side. Theirs is the task, often lonely but in the end sure of success, of calling Americans to their true destiny.

It is to be conceded that this appeal does require us to take the public seriously, even if it fails to present government as popular. It does insist on the propriety of moral judgment in public affairs even if that judgment is to be imposed on the many who are ignorant by the few who know.

Yet the Call to Public Virtue is thoroughly unsuited to provide us with the rationale we seek for popular government. It is alien to the moral actualities of American life in its account of the nature, the bearers, and the sources of its proposed public virtue. It conceives of government as a moral censor and governors a moral elite; it confounds our painfully won articulation between things religious and things political. All these it does consciously and thoughtfully, but in all it surely is in error.

Substance and Form

These authors assert the existence of a substantive public good which can be known and pursued in common action. Such a good is other than just a quality of governing, for government is only an instrument or process for pursuing such a good. The content of this good is indicated in Berns' discussion of the free speech cases in the Supreme Court. Everyone in his right mind, on Berns' premises, knows what is meant by "purity," by "loyalty," by "peaceful persuasion." But in fact the record of these cases shows how deeply men are divided on the meanings of these concepts—divided not in a confused and temporary way but on principle. It is not the case that poems, pictures, plays are equally decent or indecent to Americans young and old, urban and rural, conventional and sophisticated. It is not the case that urgent criticism of institutions or officials is in identical measure a criterion of patriotism for all Americans. It is more nearly true that there is a solid meaning for the notion of "rational" as opposed to incitatory speech, but that is precisely because it applies to the forms of action rather than the action's result.

The morality which the Call to Public Virtue proposes to instil in the American people is in fact not a morality that "everybody knows"; it is rather a morality of what "right-thinking people" know. The Call is to promote Virtue in the sense of scrubbing all our people into a well-mannered and dutiful demeanor of the sort sometimes represented in unkind caricatures of the Boy Scouts. The Call is thus deeply intemperate in its enthusiasm for virtue. In its eagerness for the right result, it ignores the crucial distinction between external expression and internal state of mind. It is a doctrine of "unlovely thoughts" or "disloyal thoughts" or "dangerous thoughts."

Exponents of the Call have been known to insist that men who think lewd thoughts have no rights under the First Amendment, that Communists and atheists can claim no rights of free expression or even due process in court, that those who think disloyally of the United States disqualify themselves for the privileges of American citizenship. Such insistences ignore the essential principle of the free mind. From the true assertion that there must be virtue in some sense in public affairs, these thinkers move on to force on others adherence to their own private notions of virtue.

It is strange indeed to read Hallowell's account of Reason's difficulties with the "merely formal element" in liberalism once the substantive support in faith was gone. Why, indeed, should Reason "drift"? Acknowledgment of moral quality in one's fellow-citizens, however attended by recognition of differing religious or economic or aesthetic standards, has no necessary implications for "drift," any more than has the recognition within a family that there is a good for adults and another for growing children. In fact these new conservatives themselves deny respect for morality by insisting upon its need for external support. The typical moral experience of Americans has been precisely the encounter, within a single polity, of differing creeds and codes. It has been an exercise, par excellence, in a morality that is formal and procedural. A government that deals fairly with the people as a whole must be, in America, one that is popular in respect of differing substantive purposes. It must not play favorites; it must not impose anyone's special moral code.

The morality that American government can embody and serve must be formal or procedural in Kant's meaning of those terms. It can include that common devotion to freedom which John Stuart Mill asserted every free modern society must require as the common object of loyalty for its people. Pursuit of candor and of impartiality and respect for a citizen's dignity are the principles that confer moral quality on a popular government, that constitute the virtue that should bless the public. Into that virtue there must flow freely the suggestions, the importunities, of each and every school of private virtue. Any man who thinks his own way good may recommend it even to those who believe it fraught with death.[13] Of course enthusiasts always try to share their goods with others. But

the true public virtue of a democracy resists alike the substantive enthusiasms of excess love and excess antipathy—of
those who exploit the public machinery either to convert or
to destroy.

There is a pathos of insecurity in Hallowell's account of
"Reason's drift" after it was "cut loose from its moorings" in
faith. He fears, it seems, that obedience to right doctrine can
be assured only by force, that true distinctions between excellence and mediocrity will not come out, that those of unusual refinement or thoughtfulness will be pulled down by
envy and detraction. This is indeed a lack of faith, of faith in
the superiority of reason, of faith in the power of good to
command popular recognition.

And it is lack of faith, too, in the power of the rational
imagination in public policy. The new conservative is unable
to distinguish the educational policies properly imposed upon
the young from those indirect and legitimate procedures in
which the natural common aspirations of adult citizens may
find expression.

It has been intellectually fashionable for some decades to
criticize the "formal" approach to ethics and politics.[14] Yet the
lesson of our present situation is that such an approach is
the only one compatible with popular government. We are
not, as a people, responsive to suggestions that would impose
upon the public at large the tenets of Puritan codes or Catholic
codes or those of any other private group. As a people, we
have tolerance beaten or weathered into us insofar as we have
not been rationally persuaded of it. The problem of public
morality is how to maintain such tolerance without so attenu-
ating our common agreement that it fails to endow our public
enterprise with any moral significance. Those who sound the
Call to Public Virtue hold that not only common procedures
but additional common ends as well are requisite for this. They
fail to understand that forms and procedures can be, in the
crucial sense, themselves the ends of common behavior. Anything is an end which action seeks, and if the form of an
action is temporally or psychologically secondary, this does

not mean that it cannot be practically an end of primary importance.

There is genuine practical meaning in asserting that a given style of conduct can be a moral end. To advise an individual or a meeting to be self-governing is to prescribe a significant end, in clear distinction from particular projects undertaken. Of course, no formal end is sought apart from substantive undertakings. And there can be real tensions of loyalty between formal and material principles. But as we attend to form or process we need not be committing ourselves to moral shadows or trivia. The ends which Kant envisioned for his ideal society can associate in kingly fashion without derogation of the earthly projects in which their association is manifest.

Kant's name is so thoroughly identified with "moralism to excess" that a comment is in order on the true import of the Kantian doctrine. Kant was indeed insistent on the primacy of duty. He stressed the difference between the moral and non-moral elements in human nature; he stipulated that there be no qualification on the ascendancy of the moral. But if it was to be the better part of one's nature that must rule, it still must be one's own nature and not that of someone else. Kant was not, like the new improvers, so impatient of vice as to be disrespectful of liberty. Doubtless, as Mr. Justice Holmes observed in his *Abrams* dissent, to one who is sure of the way to salvation persecution seems "perfectly logical."[15] But Kant did not, any more than most twentieth-century Americans, believe in persecution. He did not believe that we can keep others' souls from perdition by external sanctions. He knew that the only way to "save" others, beginning with our own children and friends, is to communicate "true doctrine" so as to commend it to their independent minds. It is this style of moral communication that is essentially formal, and this Kant defended precisely because of the intensity of his moral concern for human dignity.

To this we may add that although Kant in fact set forth in his political theory the principles of the so-called negative or night-watchman state, that theory admits of a more positive construction. Between the fully coercive and fully permissive relations between government and governed there is the great range of informing and coordinating activities by government. Rationality in the citizen need not be advanced simply by the government's doing nothing. A modern government can fulfil immense responsibilities in educational and economic fields without impairing the freedom of its citizens.

THE UNCOMMONLY VIRTUOUS

The second basic failing of the Call to Public Virtue is its insistence on restricting political authority to men specially qualified in terms of that Virtue. It is stipulated that our rulers must be wise in that Virtue, confident of that wisdom, eager to diffuse it. Rossiter indeed, in describing the philosophy of the Federalist Papers as the finest "true Conservatism," disclaims any conviction about "elites of men who can be angels."[16] But the persistent habit of the men whom he associates with American conservatism has been the identification of a special group whose mission is to advance the morality of the rest of the people. From the Boston seventeenth-century hierarchy through John Adams' "natural aristocracy" and Calhoun's restriction of liberty to the "intelligent, patriotic, virtuous and deserving," down to the school of Leo Strauss, we find recurrent the theme of elite rule. In practice, as de Tocqueville noted, American conservatives have not been blatant about this belief, but in their hearts they have stubbornly maintained that the "better" should govern the rest—that the rest cannot really be self-governing.

The conservatives affirm a necessary conflict between provisions for excellence in government and the adherence to principles which are consistent with the self-government of all. They deny the possibility of a fundamental congruity between the moral conceptions of those who are chosen to rule and those who choose them; they reject the completely open competition in which the rules are comprehended by everyone.

The Call to Public Virtue is committed to the distinction between the Few Who Know and the Many Who Should Not

Try to Know. The position goes beyond the thesis that only good men can know the good. It proclaims orders of goods, with the higher ones accessible only to persons of uncommon elegance and cultivation. Only the Virtuous are really Called. And this is why they cannot hope to speak for the broad mass of the people. The esoteric goodness they preach could not prevail in our society without intolerable compulsion. Though our "mass culture" may be low in quality, we will hardly elevate it by imposing by fiat any special standard expressing a private taste. Though we regret irrationality, we do not reduce it by an indiscriminate use of force against it. Public morality is not to be planted in us by a corps of priestly initiates. An elite contemptuous of the masses will not improve them, even if the effort helps the elite to forget its own futility.

The criteria in terms of which rulers are properly to be identified are indeed "formal"—they include devotion to the national well-being and willingness to take thought so as to inform that devotion. Through such criteria a common basis for mutual judgment can be provided; such seem indeed the principles of selection postulated by educators as diverse as Plato and Jefferson. Such a combination of the "spirited" and "rational" elements is a fair basis for distinction, surely, and still it is consistent with radical differences in more particular ethical standards. Those variations in sensitivity, in energy, in subtlety, ambition, and endurance which are the root of personal differences are quite compatible with a recognition of common standards and of a fundamental equality in responsiveness to those standards. The only admissible elite in a democracy is one which can rationally justify itself to everyone else.

RELIGION AND PUBLIC MORALITY

The culminating objection to the Call to Public Virtue is the way in which it invokes the support of religion. It is true that Americans always have tended to associate religion with politics; the Stouffer committee reported in 1954 that the principal objection of typical Americans to Communism is to its "godlessness."[17] On occasion we find a justice of the Supreme Court declaring that our institutions presuppose a Supreme Being,[18] though the same justice had indeed said in an earlier case that the Founding Fathers made "man's relation to God no concern of the state."[19] Again a recurrent saying, in the context of both international tensions and domestic problems, is that we are after all a religious nation.

We surely can be a religious nation without bringing religion into politics. The Supreme Court, though hardly with unanimity or full clarity, has been coming to say that in recent decisions. It is saying, as in cases involving public school prayers and Bible reading, that religion may be the foundation of morality without being on that account a specific guide for political action. Public schools and other public institutions are not the proper media for religious instruction. One can teach the duties of the citizen without reference to religion. In this there is neither praise for nor hostility to religion. But there is the declaration that the source of political standards may be found in men's awareness of their right relations with other men. It is such awareness that prescribes "equal treatment" regardless of creed.

The true friend of religion is the man who accords to religion the ways of persuasion appropriate to religion, and these are the ways of intellectual or "inner" persuasion. They are not the ways of public pressure. Those who urge public support for religious orthodoxy, or just for "religion in general," forget the nature of the religious process in their eagerness for the religious result. They conceive of faith as verbal adherence to conventional doctrine. In so doing they become themselves the genuine opponents of serious religion.

The critical weakness of the conservative argument, in the American context, may be seen in its appeal to a "higher law." Hallowell and Strauss insist that all moral obligations ultimately must be derived from "fact," from that eternal Is which consists in an attitude or expression of divinity. To this "metaphysical fallacy"[20] Americans have in practice always responded that moral freedom involves a clear disjunction between what is and what ought to be. Divinity is no doubt as it should be, but this does not mean that its goodness is dependent on its existence. Anything that Americans have been or are is only a limiting condition on what they ought to be. American tradition itself is noble and worthy, but it is not therefore immune to criticism. Of any actual object, natural or human, one always may ask "Is it good? Can it be better? What should I do about it?" The question is especially appropriate in an America where the frontier called for continual refreshing of the cultural heritage. Moral judgments of course "take account of fact," but they are not bound by fact. Authentic freedom consists in response to obligation whatever the facts may be.

The morality which informs our political life may be religious but need not be religious. To raise the question is no concern of the political authorities. Atheists, agnostics, true believers may qualify for testimony in courts or voting or holding public office. The proper basis for judging them is their practical dedication to democratic forms of behavior. They may communicate to one another, privately, the force and content of their own religious creeds, their own convictions of the world's and men's "ultimate nature," but this process is corrupted as soon as friendly persuasion is replaced by coercion. The Supreme Court has rightly declared the First Amendment absolute in respect of the free exercise of religion.

THE PRAISE OF THE PRIVATE ASSOCIATION

The alternative to asserting a substantive public morality as the basis for a popular government may logically be found by looking in the opposite direction. To be securely popular, say the empirically minded, we must begin from those indubitable centers of spontaneous moral activity—the local and voluntary associations. There may be a problem in connecting these with one another and with the government. But we will have the advantage of at least starting with material that is verifiable, accessible to common observation.

The empirical approach to political morality has been pursued at the level of popular discussion and also of theoretic statement. Both of these date from about the turn of the

century, when "science" was carrying forward in the social
field that campaign which already had carried the day in
physics and biology. At the popular level America produced
in the muckrakers an earnest school of investigators who insisted that we must find our political values in research "from
the ground up." The somewhat unlovely reference to the basic
material may be considered evidence of the investigators' sensitivity rather than of pessimism about the values that might
be elicited. In any case, since Lincoln Steffens,[21] sentiment has
been strong for the study of our standards in no strange land
but right here. Since Steffens there has been a determined
school of reporting, sceptical of theoretic morals, and devoted
to sniffing out the terrain at close range. The hound dog,
though keen of nose, need not be farsighted, and this empiricism may have trouble getting off the ground. But in its own
way it is associated with a normative view which, though
cautiously stated, is general in import.

These empiricists see before their eyes men forming associations—families, companies, unions, clubs. They form these
"voluntarily," to attain specific private ends. Indeed, the
voluntary and private aspects are thought to be virtually
equivalent: "private" means not only "what concerns me
alone" but also "what I do with as I will." Associations with
these qualities clearly are desired and are therefore good; they
are good, too, externally in that none is too powerful. Praise
of such private associations appears, as in some of the older
individualist theories, to propose a moral division of labor
which locates virtue in such private circles, leaving unvir-
tuous and expediential tasks to public machineries. Such was
Steffens' implication as he reveled in the eminence "bad men"
achieved in American politics. In his view, "good men"
restricted themselves to private business, "bad men" func-
tioned in the public arena, and the wise observed both and
influenced neither. At present the private associations also are
represented as our special antitotalitarian weapon, our defense
against the state's "monopoly of force." In an interesting
application to labor, Seymour Lipset and others have argued
that the shining example of "democratic unionism"—the In-

ternational Typographical Union—is uniquely characterized by a multitude of internal voluntary associations. Such groups —social, athletic, intellectual—are thought to deflect energies from an obsessive concern with the central organization; they help to forestall conflict that might become civil war.

At the level of political theory this school of thought affirms allegiance to Federalist Paper Ten,[22] though with, I believe, less than adequate attention to the rhetorical problems which occasioned Madison's special emphasis in that classic text. Madison phrased his problem as that of the "factiousness" of private associations, especially as these were related to public affairs. But factions were a problem only in the context of a public good "above faction" and above private good. Support from his argument for the Praise of the Private Association has been drawn from his claim that the new "extended republic" could—by its extent—prevent factious groups from forming dangerous majorities. There must be liberty for groups to form, but they would be balanced by others. It would be only in small communities like Rhode Island that a single faction like the debtors could convulse the whole society.

Current empirical theory, confronting the totalitarian specter, has shifted emphasis to the role of interest groups as a defense against overpowerful government. In part this defense has been conceived mechanically—the groups stand between individual and government. But again it is claimed that the groups are the basic elements in the development of the capacity for self-government. Primary loyalties, primary moral experiences, are found in families, schools, companies, unions, churches; the state, if an interest group at all, is latent and secondary. If government is popular, it is so only remotely. Per contra, as Arthur Schlesinger argued in his "Biography of a Nation of Joiners," voluntary associations are the "fundamental cement of national integration."[23]

As these thinkers formulate their approach to politics, they invoke, as noted above, the spirit of "science," a science that begins in "facts" and consciously refrains from "independent" judgments of value in the course of analysis, though not always in its conclusion. In this scientific effort the school comes under severe criticism from Professor Strauss and his associates,[24] who demand that the study of politics start with an account of what a good society is, what a good man is, and how a good man is to be governed. The empiricists decline to begin from this explicitly normative basis: they attempt rather to identify observable units of political behavior, to classify them, and to discover their characteristic modes of interaction. Only after a dependable structure of terms and propositions is developed, they say, will it be possible to offer instructions for policy. And only then will there be assurance that such instruction has not been prejudiced by some initial bias.

An impressive example of the empirical theory at work is afforded by Professor David Truman's *The Governmental Process*. The main body of the book is devoted to studying the functioning of various groups within the American political system. The discussion is "behavioral" in that it focuses upon groups "from the outside," as they form, seek equilibrium, gain it, keep it, lose it, regain it, or perhaps disintegrate. It is only in the final chapter that Truman turns to ask what these groups mean for American democracy. Then he becomes expressly normative. He asks: "Is the operation of these groups good for democracy?" "Does it lead to division, to stability, to recurrent malignancy?" "How does it influence the democratic mold, that pervasive condition which affects all groups but it is not constitutive of a group itself?" In dealing with such questions, Truman clearly is answering the "value-laden" inquiries of those who seek instructions for policy.[25]

The treatment which Truman accords to descriptive and normative categories has met sharp criticism from the Strauss group. In *Essays on the Scientific Study of Politics*, Professor Leo Weinstein devotes a chapter to "The Group Approach: Arthur F. Bentley," and much of his discussion is aimed at Truman. As Weinstein reads him, Truman is confused and inconsistent in the way he introduces political norms into his analysis: in terms of Truman's basic starting point, Weinstein claims, any normative argument was made irrelevant. But Weinstein makes this point only by ascribing to Truman, as to "Bentleyans" in general, a positivist exclusiveness which admits the propriety of nothing but descriptive statements about verifiable and measurable entities. The new conservatives tend to phrase all arguments in metaphysical terms, and it is characteristic of them to insist upon an irreducible conflict between a political theory that starts with "goods" and any other theories which—not having expressly started with normative judgments—never can introduce them. In this, they read the opposing theories oversimply. Truman does not, as I read him, deny the "reality" of "political norms." Rather, he offers a behavioral account of such norms in terms of frequency and relation to other behaviors: a norm is roughly a rule of equilibrium—the quality of an activity's termination. This might be the corollary of a merely descriptive and thoroughly mechanical principle of political value. But it need not be. It is consistent with other principles of value. On this point I think that the conservatives have raised a false issue. Truman is not really divorcing fact from value in any sense that would render the study of the former irrelevant to judgments in terms of the latter.

When Truman announces that his data are the behaviors of human groups, he is not denying that such groups aim at certain ends or that the ends can be systematized. He is not saying, "Let us stop judging political behaviors." He is saying only, as I understand him, that any political factor which has causal efficacy must be the same kind of being as that which causes. Politics, as overt human transactions, is not the issue of an ineffable and indiscoverable spirit. Truman's motive, like that of the post-Hegelians generally, thus is to eliminate the unverifiable from political theorizing. But there are norms and purposes which can be verified in the sense that they can be seen to direct behavior.

There is a related problem which confronts Truman's analysis, and which is indeed difficult for Truman to answer. This is the problem of the transcendence by the standards in genuine normative criticism of anything directly experienced or given. I believe that this is a valid objection to the behaviorists, but as I explained above it seems to me to hold against the conservatives as well. They in the end, and rather more explicitly than the liberals, appear to merge value and fact and to make moral criticism a form of cosmic ratification of what Is.

It is my own belief that political study is best initiated within a normative framework, and this is what I attempt here as I ask how a morally popular government can be understood and promoted in American society. But so to start does not require a drastic exclusion of "facts" or of "particulars" or of "everyday experience." The conservatives claim this only because they are unable to understand that studying moral principles in their context need not reduce the principles to the context. It is in fact useful to consider the aspect of principles like self-government in their local appearances, and this we can profitably explore by following some of Truman's argument in *The Governmental Process*.

Truman's major premise is that for all "human organisms," the "limitations, aspirations and values that each holds will have developed in relation to the groups with which each has early been associated."[26] Such groups exert an influence more direct than does the society as a whole. This does not necessarily confer on the groups a higher value than that of the society, but it does appear to establish a dynamic priority which is congenial to such a rating. It appears to set limits to the range of values which may be attached to a government that is popular. A self-governing people may need to break the violence of faction, but it cannot be fundamentally hostile to the impulses that animate special interest groups. These impulses frame and condition men's responsiveness to government.

The group activities are primary in analysis because they are, as Bentley claimed, the primary verifiable data which actually are presented in human interactions. Not private minds, nor group minds, but palpable associated behaviors by and among men are the proper data for the student of government. Individuals may be identified, but only in terms of biological differences, or by the facts of overlapping memberships—individuals are what groups share. There is such a thing as a state or whole society, but this is known only as a potential or actual expression of a shared interest. Groups form and contend in terms of achieving, preserving or restoring the equilibrium necessary to sustain them. Government is to be understood in terms of its relation to this equilibrium.

More explicit discussion is devoted to government and the whole society when Truman turns in his last chapter to meet the claim that the great variety of groups must engender confusion, which will in turn produce a trend toward "a man on a white horse." Such a trend is offset, Truman argues, by the balancing influence of overlapping memberships in various groups and of "membership in those potential groups based upon interests held widely through the society."[27] Distinction is here expressly drawn between actual interest groups which directly engage men's wills and "potential" groups which may even include all men concerned with law and order. Though Truman is not completely explicit on this point, it seems fair to say that he locates primary political value in the voluntary interest groups and accords a secondary value to the society as a whole. As I read him, Truman does not affirm a difference in kind between the claims of public and of private groups. Each and every interest fairly asserts its claim. And these claims supply, as the groups seek equilibrium in their various ways, the materials from which America's popular morality is to be formed. The important differences between the claims are matters of degree, reflecting closeness to or distance from the primary groups.

THE PRAISE MUTED

My own quarrel with this analysis involves the status which appears assigned to the claims of the public. I read Truman's account of the public as latent or potential, his somewhat cautious identification of the "democratic mold" as implying a secondary status in normative terms. From his beginning with the norms most accessible to immediate observation he appears to argue that what is less perceptible is less important.

But the most near need not be the most dear. We can, more sharply than he has done, distinguish psychological from ethical remoteness; we can discover that in a social complex where all interests are somewhat actual, somewhat potential, the latter may in fact supply conditions for the former. We may show, from the inner dynamic of the private associations, how an effective and popular government is both required and justified. We may manage to develop explicitly the sense in which it is true that, as Truman puts it, "guardianship will emerge out of the affiliations of the guardians."[28]

PLURALITY NEEDS UNITY

There is little doubt that our private associations at their best are indeed "popular," although they normally become oligarchic, especially as they outlive their initial vitality.[29] In general, in present-day America, the claims of our public association lack the moral power of the private associations. In the latter, we think, we live as we will; to the former we concede as we must. Our problem is to clarify the continuities that link the two. It is a problem which the social contract theory approached in terms of the whole society and individual and answered by seeing the society as the issue of a grand concert of individual wills. Some contemporary syndicalists are inclined to substitute private groups for the individuals of that older theory, to conceive of society as the group of groups, the association of associations. But this separates the individual from the whole society more sharply than is compatible with an adequate relation between him and his government. Individuals are denied effective association with one another in national terms.

The school of thought whose first enthusiasm is the private association—as duly purified of factiousness—sees government as a morally neutral adjuster of the claims of the various associations. That government does in fact play such an adjusting role no one can deny. But this school does not, in its own terms, offer a principle for the adjusting. It lacks a theory by which to formulate one group's standing relative to that of others. It urges that each of us belong to many groups lest we become too passionate about any one, but it has no specific against schizophrenia. The theory in fact assumes, almost as earnestly as did the believers in natural right, a kind of pre-established moral harmony which will keep such associations, *if rightly understood,* from overassertion. Thus the theory neglects the tensions generated by the partial character of the associations. It ignores the problem of finding a single man in a charitable churchgoer, a prudent entrepreneur, a gentle father, a strenuous veteran, a competitive golfer, a sociable Rotarian. It welcomes the star-spangled display of personality which Plato foresaw in his account of the "democratic man." It affirms the equality of each and every interest in a way which has little to do with the way in which men, as distinct from whimsies, truly are equal. If overlapping memberships moderate political passions, they also, in themselves, generate personal perplexities. In the face of "pluralism" like this, it is hardly surprising that there has been a reaction in the name of a peremptory authority.

More important, however, is the fallacy of conceiving the private association as moral in a way that the public association is not. It is not the case that the private association is fully voluntary, the public entirely coercive. Private associations are themselves in varying degrees private governments. There is no pure monopoly of force in society. There may be only one agency that is "strongest"—one that lawfully may kill. But there are many which practically can starve or confine men. Coercion of man by man is ubiquitous. In matters that count the most—the fulfilment of capacity, the enrichment of everyday life, the mobility we need for freedom of economic choice—we are hedged about and limited by many groups smaller than the whole society. Corporations, unions, clubs, schools all exert decisive influence. They are not simply what we make them; they are mainly as we find them; and they go far to make us what we are. To this extent they are, as Dewey said, themselves public; they determine willy-nilly the character of men's careers in the society at large.

Political behavior is found not only in governments but also in all situations where men associate and affect one another

in ways that are in some sense "official." Groups are found
acting politically; individuals act politically too, and so do
whole societies. Any one of these can be said to organize into
a single course of action a number of tendencies toward fulfilment. The variations they exhibit in frequency and in integration do not justify regarding some of them as unreal or
secondary. Official government's role may be sometimes less
clear or prominent than that of private governments, but in
principle it is the kind of role which is susceptible of greater
prominence and greater power.

Recognition of the dynamic continuum of private and public
associations leads to acknowledgment that they are morally
continuous as well. Neither is mere will or mere force; in both,
force is exerted on behalf of a purpose more or less articulate.
There is no more reason for government to be unpopular,
uncongenial to the governed, than for an association to be
unpopular. Both kinds of groups reflect in varying measure
not only eager will and necessitous compulsion but also the
softer influences of habit and social approval. Of course a
stupid or oppressive government may be made less stupid, or
more tolerant, by the resistance of a resolute and morally inte-
grated private association. Equally, a stubborn and factious
private group may thwart and confuse the advancement of
a broad program in the public interest.

To speak of private and public associations as morally con-
tinous is not to assert a necessary harmony. Nor is it to deny
official government's priority in the sense that it can and must
define the conditions within which the private associations
function, including their internal structures. Even to utter
this thought at present—unless one directs it at Communists,
or the most palpably "corrupt" unions—is to appear to applaud "totalitarian" assaults on private groups, to approve
the oppressions of the "mass society." But these oppressions
are the work of a government that is deservedly unpopular.
Such a government naturally results from failure to accord it
the respect due to a vehicle of the common will. Extrapolation
from German and Russian totalitarianism has gone far to
obstruct serious thought on American politics; we differ from

European countries significantly in our flexibility and our readiness to form new associations. We have achieved, despite the incomplete character of our public activity, tolerably adequate representation in government of our principal private interests.

UNITY FROM PUBLICITY

The linkage which holds together private and public associations as continuous is, in our political usage, the establishment of frank and responsible communication. On one side it is the process of political petition, agitation, "lobbying"; on the other it is investigation, revelation, bringing to public view those activities in which the public has a legitimate interest. The dramatic import of such communications is confirmed by Truman in his observation that "a simple increase in knowledge often has the effect of defining and activating an interest group."[30]

The problems of the limits and worth of specific lobbying or investigatory activities are only special examples of the general problem of how far government may and should concern itself with the internal affairs of interest groups—economic, academic, or religious. Does government rightly insist that union officers must—if the union is to invoke the offices of the National Labor Relations Board—complete non-Communist affidavits? Should students who receive government financial aid be required to disclose all of their political interests and aspirations? May a union or a private school or college be required to show whether or not it discriminates against racial or religious minorities? May a professional group enjoying quasi-public status—the bar or the doctors—be required to show that it governs itself by accepted democratic procedures? To such questions it seems clear that we cannot reply simply by telling government to "stay out." That cannot be what freedom of association means. The freedom which the Constitution prescribes is a freedom which enhances and supports the freedom of others rather than restricting that freedom. To substantiate genuine freedom the government must intervene where it is necessary to protect minorities, to assure due process. Such intervention is dangerous, for any private group may exploit it as an instrument against its rivals. But with care we can avert that danger. As long as we accord any coercive power to government we need to direct and moralize its interference by bringing public opinion to bear upon it.

The private forms of association are, in the nature of the case, those in which we are less than fully responsible. Men form a church, a club, a union, a mutual benefit group, not to save the nation but to cultivate a part of it. As they share the common project they develop the self-respect and mutual confidence which mark the responsible citizen. But the very mission of the private group limits their commitment. They leave to others, or to themselves in other capacities, the question whether they are affecting adversely other limited interests and activities. The public agency finally must make the assessment of responsibility, for it alone can assume a position where it can see and act upon the social situation as a whole. Negatively, it must prevent feuds and vendettas, overt wars between private groups. Positively, it must function as a source of intelligence and inspiration to move the great complex of groups toward some intelligible unity. The government must help to bring it to pass that our city, which is many, also is one.

It is necessary and proper for the government to have a care that our private associations are "virtuous." But this is not the virtue of the school that issues the Call to Public Virtue. It is, more narrowly, such virtue as resides in responsibility, meaning ability to respond, ability to give an account of oneself. The first role of government is to see to it that the private groups give a full and frank report of their activities to the public. Such a report would have to include information on such internal structures as condition the report itself. It must be soberly exact, as the ordinary press release often is not. It would, to borrow Truman's phrase, quicken the influence within the private group of the "democratic mold"— the requirement of such arrangements as periodic elections, broad membership policies, and written constitutions.[31]

The courts are struggling currently with the question how far individuals or groups may be required to disclose information to committees of Congress or executive commissions. There is agreement that there are limits to such requirements: exposure "for exposure's sake" normally is condemned. But we are not very clear on how to draw the line between disclosure of "effective discrimination" and disclosure of "mere discriminatory preference." We think that fraud in labor unions or companies should be "exposed," but we are not entirely clear how far individuals should be protected against injustices which, in a sense, they bring on themselves. We have still to fill in much of the formula by which we will define the government's duty so to investigate as to require the private groups to promote self-government.

Government need not, surely, demand that every private association have an internal constitution exactly like that of the United States. But it may require that each be understood by its members and that those members have a chance to translate their understandings into common action. Differing purposes of course dictate different forms of internal organization. Some groups are organized tightly, some loosely. Some are, literally, "presbyterian," others "episcopalian," others "congregationalist." Some are unitary, others federated. But none is, on principle, immune from public inspection or control. There is no right of privacy when there is actual group power which affects the public. And the decisions as to when the public is affected must lie with public agencies.[32]

The *Rumely* case[33] of 1953 and that of Louisiana's recalcitrant registrars in *Hannah v. Larche*[34] in 1960 provide current illustrations of our problem. In the first there was agreement in the Supreme Court that in terms of the Lobbying Act of 1946 the identity of purchasers of books (including books on politics) fell outside the area on which testimony might legitimately be demanded by a Congressional committee. In the second case the Court divided, a majority holding that testimony could be received in the United States Civil Rights Commission on voting discriminations in Louisiana even though the identity of those who complained was not made known to those whom they accused. In the *Rumely* case a "right-wing" distributor of books and pamphlets was declared immune from having to report on his distribution list; in the *Hannah* case officials were revealed to have been charged with discrimination even though their accusers were not required to "confront" them. Earnest civil liberties advocates have been somewhat perplexed to have their heroes, Mr. Justice Black and Mr. Justice Douglas, agree with the *Rumely* decision and dissent in *Hannah*.

There are two principles at work in these cases—the freedom of political discussion and the requirement of due process. In the *Rumely* case, compulsory disclosure was judged to invade freedom of political discussion, though the Court conceded that such protection would not be available for a lobbyist trying to influence votes in Congress directly. On the other hand, in *Hannah v. Larche*, the accusations against the registrars were allowed to remain in the records of the federal Civil Rights Commission because the Court's majority, over the dissents of Black and Douglas, asserted that due process could be assured the registrars without identifying and exposing to community reprisals the Negroes who had testified against the registrars in the commission's closed hearings. The majority appear to assume that the absence of witnesses might be relevant in any assessment of the merits of the testimony in a legal proceeding.

These Supreme Court decisions, then, affirm the following propositions about the power of government to compel publicity: (1) in the general domain of reading and buying and selling books we are committed to unimpeded expression or action about which testimony may not be compelled; (2) in such communication as is identified as "lobbying," such as that involved in a direct approach to a legislator about legislation, the identity and resources of a lobbyist must be made known to the public; and (3) though clearly due process of law requires much in the way of disclosure, to the public and to accused persons, it does not require—as in the voting cases in Louisiana—identification of witnesses who cannot be assured protection from reprisal. The latter is not to be associated with the thesis that voting rights are more important than due process of law; rather, in the *Hannah* case, it is believed due process can be assured without disclosure. Had this not been true, and had appropriate publicity been essential to due process, then government would have had to associate with disclosure measures adequate to protect the witnesses.

SELF-KNOWLEDGE AS CONSTITUTIVE OF THE PUBLIC

At one extreme in political theory we have our "overmoral" writers, who will have "the good," whatever the facts; at the other extreme are the "realists," who must start from the facts, whatever the moralities. The first seek the impossible and deplore the government that fails to supply it; the second make little demand upon government, morally, but accept its exploitation for unstated ends. The Call to Public Virtue demands of our political institutions that they diffuse the morality appropriate to our small and intimate groups; its adherents become angry or resigned when the prescription is ignored. If they decide to inquire into the situation, they do not know how to stop short of Inquisition. The Praise of the Private Association, also taking its start from nonpublic activities, asserts that government's ends are not truly moral ends; it accepts the shrewd pursuit, in the public domain, of private ends which are not publicly acknowledged; it has really no rationale for accumulating knowledge to inform policy.

The theory of a truly popular government, which can responsibly initiate and direct the public's self-knowledge, must conceive government as at once the instrument of force and the expression of will. Our governing, which must be effective, also must pursue virtue. But this is not the substantive virtue prescribed by the neoclassicists. Its range is limited to the formal qualities of honesty and consistency and above all of candor. The First Commandment, like the First Amendment, of our Constitution is that our government should help us to keep aware of what we are doing—doing as one com-

munity and also as a collection of smaller communities. This
is not government's only role. But it is its most important role
—its constitutive role. For the energetic pursuit of definite
common interests and loyalties at the local and private levels
can be consistent with the freedom of all only if there is
common understanding of what groups and individuals are
doing to one another. The constitution of ourselves as a self-
governing community involves this self-knowledge above
all. It is the condition of genuine fellowship in distinction
from undiscriminating mass enthusiasm.

It is a measure of our incompleteness that though we celebrate the classic wisdom of Plato and Aristotle we accord little
serious attention to their vision of rulers authentically
equipped with political wisdom. This is not simply because
we are democratic and resist the fusion of political power and
wisdom in a limited group of men. Rather, we are sceptical
about being able to find such wisdom. We have indeed not
found very much. Our government is the repository of an immense collection of data, military, social, economic. But most
of this wins little exposure to public view, is under little pressure to assume the integrity that can make it suitable for
guidance of public policy. We have not lived with it long
enough and intimately enough to effect its translation into
terms that will permit public judgment of it, that will enable it
to inform the public judgment too.

We who are college professors usually can talk to one another in such a vein without embarrassment, provided we
avoid such sensitive topics as the admissions policies of our
own institutions or the private interests of our own departments. To commend the development of "common knowledge"
to associations of American business and labor is less easy. The
task is to make popular exactly what is unpopular in America
today. It is to achieve recognition of the fact of private government wherever men are associated. It is then to insist that such
government be responsive to the kinds of community demands
that are a matter of course for our elected public officials. It
is further to refuse to abandon to purely "private knowledge"
that which is necessarily public in impact. In the great com-

munity, that which is of public moment must be known by
the public.

THE GOOD SOCIETY OF WALTER LIPPMANN

The discussion of moralistic and realistic strains in American
political theory may fairly be summed up by reference to that
highly informed and serious commentator, that interesting
conservative who so often voices liberal opinions—Mr. Walter
Lippmann. Lippmann's position has changed somewhat over
the years; it is his view as stated in the 1930's that I shall
discuss here.

In *The Good Society* Lippmann criticized both the New
Dealers and their opponents. The former, in their enthusiasm
for planning, were committing themselves to decisions that
must be arbitrary. The latter, notably in the conservative Supreme Court, were resisting the New Deal's social legislation
in the name of an indefensibly rigid interpretation of property
as a natural right. In fact, Lippmann claimed, government
should limit itself to the supremely important task of pre-
venting arbitrariness in human relations. Government may
regulate contracts and the enjoyment of property; indeed, government may regulate any conduct. But government always
must respect the inviolability of the human person. That is
the higher law—the central theme of "true conservatives"—
which men have slowly and painfully come to recognize.

It was Lippmann's special concern, in the face of the "collectivism" of the 1930's, to show that economic planning must
be arbitrary. It asserted common objectives in an area where
no common objectives can be found. "Anyone can imagine an
enemy and hate him, . . . but to talk about an abundant life
is merely to begin an interminable argument."[35] Government
can have no sure principles for making such economic decisions. The system of natural liberty is the only one which
can avoid arbitrariness; the New Deal's gradual collectivism
is only a series of piecemeal favors to interest groups. The
best that government can do is to be an impartial adjuster of
competing claims and guardian of liberty for all.

If readers of Lippmann's *Public Opinion* had thought they

detected there a disposition favoring philosopher-rulers, they were in *The Good Society* admonished to think otherwise. No one is wise enough to legislate substantively for a society's future—to decide economic priorities. The New Dealers ignored the higher law to which all governments are subject. They were indeed reacting against a specious appeal to higher law: Lippmann conceded that conservatives had, since the Civil War, perverted economic freedom into an alleged natural freedom of contract. Lippmann thus supported New Dealers like Thurman Arnold in their complaint that "the pioneer liberals . . . vindicated" a law "which was in many respects the mere defense of ancient privileges and immunities."[36] But it was Lippmann's contention that "liberalism" in the specifically economic sense could be disentangled from its historic associations. "The denial that men may be arbitrary in human transactions *is* the higher law," he wrote. "By this higher law all formal laws and all political behavior are judged in human societies."[37]

Walter Lippmann has been conspicuously successful, in a distinguished career, in focusing general considerations upon problems of public policy. The principle he formulates is not a substantive moral law such as that advocated by the new conservatives. The principle is not easy to make precise: Lippmann asserts it to be a "progressive discovery of men striving to civilize themselves."[38] This higher law against arbitrariness thus is conceived as an expression of what men, in their troubled collisions, have been trying to realize. The principle is formal; it is a rule for adjusting the claims of men and groups. Government is the great adjuster, always open to challenge in terms of this higher law.

I believe that Lippmann was in error in likening the New Deal to totalitarian regimes in its planning efforts; I think that in the great complex of effective planning in our society government can play a vital though not exclusive role. That role is, I believe, broader than that prescribed in Lippmann's political theory.

Lippmann urged in *The Good Society*[39] that democratic government should be conceived as adjusting claims, not as issuing commands. There surely is much adjustment for government to carry out in the face of the clamor arising from our larger and smaller private governments. But government must be more than adjuster or judge. Government should not simply await the rising up of assertions or disputes. Government must always be concerned about whether self-government and the conditions of self-government are being maintained. Government must take the initiative. Again, government cannot please everyone. Some get less than they want and must accept it. In this sense government must command— even a popular government.

Government's initiative must be shown, notably, in the enterprises of education and of conservation; these are, quite as much as justice, the concern of a democratic government. The education to be sought is precisely that which will enable men to live dependably in a regime of law. The suggestion may seem ominous: Lippmann observed that in Plato's kind of society the effort would be made to "re-create men to fit the design."[40] But in fact in our society men are being re-created all the time. If their characters are "their own business," this does not exclude government from helping them to grow. In education government can provide the instruments and materials which are, in distinction from whips and scorpions, the appropriate aids to free men who are trying to become civilized.

Again, a modern democratic government must undertake the conserving of natural and humanly created beauty, as well as of all those natural resources which may be identified as bestowed upon the society "in common." There are indeed difficulties about exactly what these are. But we make decisions about conservation for military purposes, and in principle the same kind of logic might apply to what we need for times of peace. In fact education and conservation are continuous: in areas like the maintenance of adequate health standards they merge.

Government must, then, be active in ways which Lippmann seemed unwilling to approve. How active government should be is a question which turns upon the dimensions of the social and economic groups that are active. Were we to restrict ourselves to indefinitely small units, Lippmann's actual prescription might be suitable. But as it is, the government which we commission to assure impartiality must take the initiative. It will no doubt collide with private groups: witness our difficulties in moving with peace and decisiveness in respect of racial segregation. But collisions are tolerable if they are handled with firmness and humor. If, as Lippmann says, "the gradual encroachment of true law upon wilfulness and caprice is the progress of liberty in human affairs,"[41] a modern government is not barred from promoting that encroachment, so long as all the people have a chance to help form that policy.

Lippmann centers his theory on judges. Though he was critical of the anti-New Deal Supreme Court for its appeal to a rigid view of property, still it seems that in the main he put his trust for adherence to the higher law in the judicial dispensation. Coke was his hero, confronting the Scottish James I with the legacy of the English common law. But the task of the modern governor must be wider than good judgment. The task involves much more than knowledge of common law development—more than, in America, knowledge of constitutional development. The task truly is the one Rousseau assigned to the Founders, the men he called "Legislators." It is the task of divining the cultural spirit and intent of the people, of determining in what special ways their talents may unfold and mature. It is a task for the concert of the best energies— judicial, executive, legislative, academic, poetic, managerial— that we can muster.

If this statement only repeats what is contained in Lippmann's argument, so much the better. I think that his objections to New Deal economic policies pushed him into a view of government more limited than is consistent with government's being truly popular. He moved from the "night-watchman state" to the "judicial state" but stopped short of a genuinely "positive state," an affirmative instrument of common intentions. He spoke of liberty primarily in terms of reducing arbitrary government. Thus he recited the story of the persecutions visited upon inquirers like Galileo. It is possible, I think, to offer an economic analysis and an educational theory more tolerant of government initiative, without prejudice to liberty. A government that provides a school and a telescope for Galileo—yes, and national fellowships for his assistants, too—does not necessarily threaten his liberty. A people sufficiently educated about the holders of economic power may know how, without undue strain, to keep such power from becoming excessive.

POPULARITY IS NOT ENOUGH

In arguing that government must be after all the proper expression of our better selves, we run continually the danger of excess attention to ourselves, of focusing too closely on our own quality and achievement. To have our government effectively ours is indeed only significant insofar as we are worth something and have something to do, a part to play in the human enterprise. Such a part was indeed bravely delineated as the nation began; our intellectual task is to bring that delineation to bear effectively upon our operating conceptions of today.

We cannot complete that task through either dogmatic moralism or dogmatic empiricism. Neither as presently promulgated affords that rationale of public purpose which carries with it absorption in the deed to be done as distinct from the state of the doer. Nor, despite the leads he affords us, can we simply follow Walter Lippmann, particularly the rather moralistic Lippmann of such later writings as *The Public Philosophy*. The moralists are appropriately urgent about the need to be mindful of our souls, but they are overzealous for our detailed salvation. The empiricists rightly bid us live in this world but are determined to leave us severely alone in it and to have us leave one another alone, too. And Lippmann's prescriptions for the rule of law in American society are excessively hedged about with reservations as to the capacity of public agencies, except courts, to respond to the generalities that support a genuine public morality.

What America can do and can be, how deep and broad a public morality we can realize, we shall not know until we have tried ourselves—and doubtless the tests of success always will be incomplete. A popular government clearly must both govern and be popular; it must enjoy that sense of security which individuals know as they discipline their energies for serious tasks. Popularity means conformity with enduring interests and purposes; government must include the most adroit exploitation of nongovernmental momenta and interests to get the work done.

That the United States of America is one country, attempting one concerted enterprise in self-government, is in a sense the most accidental of historical developments. That the enterprise may be transformed from accident into rational and deliberate unity is not only historically possible but morally mandatory. Conceivably we may fail, but so far we have really not tried very hard. We still are taking preliminary steps toward a unity that overcomes the diversity of color, and our progress is not rapid.

Our need surely is to devise a government which is effective, discriminating, and above all active in leading us to what, in our concern for liberty, we are committed as a community to achieve. As long as government merely reacts to injustice, to outside threats, to internal corrosions, so long will government fail to attract the enthusiasms, the energies that endow it with a will of its own and maintain that will as, in essence, the common will of Americans. We need, in principle, to see what kinds of positive undertakings such a popular government may undertake; and so we shall proceed to examine government's present relations to American business and American schools.

Active Government—The People's Business
and the People's Schools

SUBSTANTIAL POPULARITY in government can be assured only
through the sense of common activity. This is not the popularity gained by the kindly giver. It is not that Santa Claus
popularity sought by every administration that wishes to remain in office. Popularity that is enduring and consistent with
self-government must issue from government's acting on the
grand scale as lesser associations and individuals act on the
narrower scale. It is the popularity that attends the public's
understanding that this is what the government is doing.

We can make this assertion concrete if we consider how
such common activities may be found in government's relation
to our economy and our education. Neither of these can fulfil
its social function without the intervention of public agencies.
The worlds of material things and mental things are held in
common by all members of society. The title that any man may
establish in either world rests, as Locke might say, on work
done and use enjoyed. If we shy from Locke's theology, still
in terms simply of human efforts and human enjoyments we
affirm the social context of our labors and our learnings. In
both of these we reckon with the moral import of government,
neither as an accident nor as a policeman, but as essential in
the process. To our different governmental agencies, in appropriate ways, we must assign responsibility for determining how
we develop and spend our resources, both natural and human.
We are not committed at large to public ownership, but we
are committed to public responsibility.

We are indeed deeply committed to private ownership, but
to an ownership which reflects less and less the older dominating conception of property in land. Spatial exclusiveness

65

lingers as a defining characteristic in terms of doors, locks, walls, strongboxes. But ownership as proprietary status is ever more clearly a social category, a relation sustained and identified in a social context. Ownership is defined and justified by its relation to public needs and public authorities.

The distinction of governmental, economic, and educational activities is elusive; our language serves us poorly. Clearly governing includes many activities which common usage terms economic or academic. We maintain in fact a number of concerted processes which we label roughly as "political," "economic," and "educational," involving, in large measure, the same persons but organized differently and pursuing different ends. Each of us may be regarded as associated with others for a number of distinct purposes—such as order, material comfort, and mental cultivation. Our problem is to see these, rightly related, in a single and coherent arrangement.

In all these processes, certainly, men may achieve or fail to achieve, may promote or impede self-government. In all we pledge ourselves more or less explicitly to obey rules attended by sanctions. It is not only in politics proper that we announce common enterprises and designate, with pride or desperation, persons commissioned to carry these through. It is not only in the political domain that we keep an ultimate power to call to account those whom we designate our agents. Holders of economic and of academic power are not sovereign. We are in fact legislators and judges ultimately of the exercise of power wherever it occurs. In this we are, to paraphrase Jefferson, all public agents, just as we are all private individuals, too. The understanding most fundamental to a self-governing society is that which concerns this interplay of public and private interests in each of us.

Most of all, such understanding requires development and diffusion of an appropriate sense of generality. We will have privacy in the proper sense only as there also is spread throughout the community the right kind of publicity. If government is to help our "nonpublic" associations to be responsible, it must make certain that the officials and members of those associations ask themselves, and are asked, the right questions. It must have authority to investigate and to compel responses. Paradoxically, a government that is to be popular must be an inquisitive government. Its pattern need hardly be set by the example of any congressional committee, but it must promote the proper studies.[1] A democratic America must have Socrates in the government as well as outside it.

Government inquires into private associations, indeed, only as the inquiry serves a proper legislative purpose. Too often in recent investigations congressional committees have assumed the guise of inquisitors who judge private individuals without being themselves responsible for assuring due process. Such a disparity reinforces the image of the private person embodying the affirmative virtues in the community and the governors as coercive. The governing bodies must be able to convey the sense that the inquiry is essential to a common important activity. A notable example of an immensely elaborate investigation of this kind was supplied by the hearings in the Senate Banking and Currency Committee on the Employment Act of 1946, ably described in Stephen K. Bailey's *Congress Makes a Law*. During the hearings there were sharp words exchanged between senators and witnesses as well as among the senators. But such disagreements were contained within the concerted study of reliable procedures for increasing the stability of the national economy. They served a public purpose.

It is a striking commentary on the divisions within our government that officials of one branch refuse on occasion to divulge information about its business to those of another branch. Given our "division of powers" this is no doubt logical. But for citizens who seek illumination on public affairs such jurisdictional secrecies are deplorable. Equally disastrous for self-government is the holding under the category of "classified" of any beyond the most rigorously defined military and diplomatic secrets. Typically, intelligence agents of other powers know much more about our government than do our citizens.

THE PRIORITY OF THE MARKET PLACE

As we consider how government is to inquire and publicize, in respect of business and the schools, we may once again take note of our presently effective folklore. In such expressions as the "people's government," the "people's business," and the "people's schools" there is a notable lack of symmetry. It is no play on words to say that the people's business is considered *theirs* in a sense which is not implied for either the government or the schools. This is not because we think a man is not busy in governing or teaching; it is not because we do not care about government or the schools; it is not because we believe that America's business is "just business." It is because to speak of a man's own business is to associate it with him in a way at once personal and private. It is to put upon the public authorities a special burden of proof in the event that they propose a public inquiry in the public interest.

Officials of government, teachers, and educational administrators do not enjoy, in our popular attitudes on these matters, the same secure base for resisting public inquiry. Indeed, when a teacher or doctor or minister wishes to challenge a public inquiry about his activities, he often responds, "This, sir, is my business and no one else's."[2] His challenge may or may not be supported in the courts, but its terms themselves rarely are attacked. Professional groups very largely have defined their relations to government in such "paraeconomic" terms: professional freedom in general and academic freedom in particular have been dominantly patterned on the style of business freedom. They have been conceived as property to be protected against public claims. They have been, often with tragic consequences, conceived as private rights rather than essential public functions.

We have, in other words, given priority to the market place; we have conceived the academy as a special and limited segment of the market place. We have in the main committed schools and colleges to government by businessmen on business principles.

A vivid picture of our traditional attitudes is presented in Robert and Helen Lynd's *Middletown in Transition*. In that account of a typical American city in the 1930's we see the leading citizens committed to steady progress in business and to tradition in education. Business was to continually refurbish the outer gear of living; the schools were to polish and acculturate the people for whom, and by whom, the living was made. Business took wing; the schools conserved. Public interference with business was the rare exception, appropriate only when progress seemed otherwise impossible. On the other hand, when schools seemed to deviate from accepted canons of belief and conduct, the public should intervene. Innovations that were "bold experiments" in business would be considered "fads" in education. There was room for continued exercise of imagination and invention in factory, trade, and farm, but the thoughts and attitudes a good school should foster already were well known. Accordingly, while intervention in the schools only restored and fortified such freedom as they should have, intervention in business truly was a restriction on freedom. In the 1960's, for all John Dewey's efforts, such educational conservatism still is very influential.

I am speaking here of attitudes of mind as well as of will— and it is in terms of business attitudes that our basic conceptions of freedom have been framed. As our market place mentality has it, if government interferes too much with schools, as by cutting pay or dictating curriculum, then the schools will react in proper measure, for example, by an exodus of teachers. Economic law will then be manifest: teacher supply falls; then teacher salaries must rise and teaching conditions improve, interference perhaps decline, and so on until once more supply meets demand. The academy is, like every other productive activity, subject to Ricardian principles, even if it is unusually prone to aberrations which require surveillance by public authorities.

GOVERNMENT AS TEACHER AND PATRON

The subordination of our academic purposes to economic goals has been disastrous to both. Our business has been made to serve a private interest conceived simply as material gain.

Our schools have promoted a vacuous community morale, or have provided a merely instrumental training or—in reaction —sought to develop a private refinement seeking elegance in isolation from the common people. The denominational schools which supplied missionaries for the home front are no longer prominent in higher education. The business schools which propose to teach thoughtfulness among executives are notable exceptions to the general practice of smoothing the way to business success. The corporations which encourage a reflective attitude toward corporate responsibility seem to take their cue from the public relations office. The institutions which nurture an American until he is of age are out of joint with those which await him as he "stands dreaming on the verge of strife." The typical American college graduate is, like Rupert Brooke, "magnificently unprepared for the long littleness of life."[3] He crosses an impressive divide as he moves from school to the "real" world of business.

Our schools and our businesses have been devoted to their respective interests—interests that are "private" in the important sense that neither has much to say to the other. Our main instrument for coming to understand ourselves has little to do, directly, with our machinery for keeping ourselves alive and healthy. If we wish to do well in one of these, it seems, we do well to pay little heed to the other. The result is tolerable, indeed, only on the premise that a man's true education comes after he has left the school.

In this situation of uneasy independence and irrelevance, it must be government's role to bring about greater continuity and understanding. We need to understand economic freedom and academic freedom so that each is a positive support to the other and to the community at large. We need, that is, to exhibit these freedoms not as the holding of government at arm's length but rather as the issue of the proper association of government with business and the schools. We must do this if we are to realize a political morality at once generous and realistic.

To the observation that two parties are at odds the friendly American response is, typically, "Well, let us make them talk, then. We'll lock them in a room and keep them there until they understand each other." The suggestion is as warm hearted as it is crude. To a sceptic it may recall the Christian martyrs and the lions. Mere juxtaposition effects no automatic conciliation. In its simplest reading the formula requires a room, a door, a lock, a key, a language. It requires a common framework and an agency to set the terms of conversation. And that framework government must supply. Economic freedom and academic freedom must be compatible with such intervention by government as will promote significant positive relations between them.

Such intervention will include compulsion. It will include, too, substantive government enterprise[4] where private effort is deficient. Essentially, government must act to maintain a proper equilibrium between business and education. In general, in our society, this means that government must supply a drastic deficiency on the academic side.

In principle the government must do two things in proper relation to one another. It must bring into business activity the best qualities of our educational practices, and it must endow education with direction from our best economic talent. Neither form of intervention is unfamiliar, but government efforts in these directions have been practiced apologetically, as a deviation tending toward mortal sin. We must understand government's educational relations with business as the natural expression of communiy concern; the business is, after all, the community's business. We need to understand government influence on education as the proper attention we give, as a public, to the development of mind and character. This is not to dissolve the distinctions between government and business and schools. It is rather to make those distinctions intelligible.

Our situation does not call for a wholly new creation of "lay boards" of directors, under government auspices, in which professors on leave will oversee business and businessmen on a dollar-a-year basis will oversee education. The educational work to be done by government, about and for the sake of business, already is being done in principle in the various government departments. What we need is an enlargement and enrichment of that system so that, whether on federal or state levels, persons expert in the social sciences and in related scientific and humanistic studies will find such work attractive as alternative to that in our colleges and universities. Such persons would be charged with public analysis and appraisal of all aspects of business activity including its impact on persons as well as other "goods."

On the other hand, we need to associate the best "business brains" of the country, more systematically than we do now, with our basic educational decisions on the dimensions and quality of our whole teaching enterprise. We need to bring those who are most sagacious about "affairs" in our culture into helping to make the crucial judgments as to how our human potential is to be developed and conserved. We need the participation of men who are secure in the sense of knowing their own development and their own status—men who escape the parochiality that besets even groups of professors and college administrators. We need men who would broadly comprehend our educational needs and the resources available to meet them. Such men would constitute, in a fundamental sense, a school board for the country.

Through such procedures we can establish a continuum in which government plays a mediating role—as public enlightener in the market place and as enterpriser among the schools. The proposal may be challenged as an effort to commit government in both areas to projects for which it is inherently unsuited. It may seem to assign the blind and the timid to leading the clever and the wilful. These objections may be valid insofar as our government is deservedly unpopular. But that unpopularity can be made to disappear if government can help us learn to reconcile our understandings in these different activities.

A government which commands popular respect may be expected to intervene in this way with eminent success. Such a government is to be understood to have available a reserve of intellectual power on the one hand and of material resources on the other. Such surely is the proper perspective on the "affluence" which is unevenly characteristic of America today. If we have the persons qualified to enlighten the public about its private economic associations, then government has the duty to develop such education in the public interest. If we have the money to build and equip schools, to encourage school teachers and students, we must not hold back because of a bogey of "government control."

The business community in America rarely has been willing to concede that government officials know enough or are responsible enough to educate business. The academic community generally has regarded government aid to education as the camel's nose that eventually will consume the entire school tent. Against my proposals here it will be argued—following our prevailing folklore—that private business should finance education and that our accepted academic institutions, together with the privately owned press, should educate us about the public import of our economic life. Without denying the wisdom of our great foundations or the independence and acuity of our best schools and newspapers, we still must recognize that they cannot alone do the job. They can do much. But they are inadequate precisely because they are private and so, in a basic sense, voluntary. We cannot assume that they will take the public stance, will pose the public questions. They cannot count on having the resources they need. Serving private interest well does not automatically serve the public. The viable American alternatives to government's owning and operating the main agencies of production and education[5] is to manage that division of labor that keeps business and the schools distinct from government but enables government to provide the conditions in which these truly will fulfil their public function. These are the dimensions in which a popular government must be active.

BUSINESS AS THE PURSUIT OF THE ORDINARY CALLINGS

American businessmen typically have been conservative in politics, and one might expect them to conceive their obligations to the public in terms of a common moral code such as that cherished by the new conservatives. In fact, business has been reluctant to accord such deference. Rather it has clung to constitutional definitions of property prevailing in the Supreme Court of the 1920's and earlier—definitions of a rigidly individualistic cast. From this perspective the country has, for more than a quarter century now, followed false doctrine. It was in 1937 that the shift of two justices determined that the federal government could intervene in major aspects of our economic life. In thus terminating a contest of over fifty years' duration, the Supreme Court formulated a tolerably clear rationale for the government's power to regulate business. The Court's opinions provide us with the basic categories for stating also the government's educational mission in the economy. And our great teacher among the Justices, even though he had retired before the final cases came to the Court, was Mr. Justice Holmes. His thinking, it is clear, deeply influenced the fundamental rulings of the 1930's.

The main outlines of Holmes' position are given in three statements, of which the earliest was his dissent in *Lochner v. New York*.[6] In deciding that New York's "labor law" regulating bakers' hours was contrary to the Fourteenth Amendment, the Court's five-man majority conceded that the freedom to hire, or to contract one's labor, might be in some circumstances subject to public restraint. But the majority, on principles which generally prevailed until the mid-1930's, found no restraint justified in Lochner's case. Their reason, Mr. Justice Holmes claimed in his dissent, was that they responded to an economic theory which they were in effect writing into the Constitution. In fact, Holmes insisted, the Constitution "does not enact Herbert Spencer's *Social Statics*" or any other theory of government's relation to business. Rather, the Constitution is in such matters indeterminate: it leaves to legislative decision the question how far government may restrict the power to enter contracts.

Mr. Justice Holmes is firmly enthroned as the Olympian sceptic about all Constitutional rigidities—and, one may add, about pretensions to Olympian majesty too. In *Tyson & Bros. v. Banton*[7] we find him remarking with characteristic irony that "the notion that business is clothed with a public interest and has been devoted to the public use is little more than a fiction intended to beautify what is disagreeable to the sufferers." Government will take what the public needs, he said, and also government will soothe. But Holmes was more than a mocking sceptic. "The truth seems to be," he continued, "that subject to compensation when compensation is due, the legislature may forbid or restrain any business when it has a sufficient force of public opinion behind it." And here Holmes supplied, if somewhat obliquely, the criterion that is moral as well as a matter of fact recognition of superior force. For though he had, doubtless, his reservations about the clarity or fairness of public opinion, he did acknowledge its validity as a basis for restricting private business. What the public regards as public is open to restriction by public agencies. This applies to labor and management, to schools, and to the press—to any business in its economic aspect. Any private economic activity is in principle open to public intervention and, a fortiori, to public inquiry.

On what grounds is the public intervention justified, and to what ends is it to be directed? Holmes answered these questions in his dissent in the Washington, D.C., minimum wage case in 1923, *Adkins v. Children's Hospital*.[8] In rejecting the Court majority's conclusion that a minimum wage law unduly abridged the freedom of contract, Holmes asserted that in earlier and, as he thought, wiser interpretations of the due process clause there had been no more than an "unpretentious assertion of the liberty to follow the ordinary callings." The phrase is rather quaint. It requires the stature of Holmes to commend to our reading of the Constitution a concept central to a religious tradition in which Holmes was reared and on which he directed his detached and sceptically independent criticism. But the phrase offers the formula, however broad, for the principle which legitimates public intervention in and public revelation about our economic life.

The liberty to follow the ordinary callings is associated with an expectation that talents will be employed where they are useful, where they are in demand. The "calling" is not to virtue, directly, but to a job of interest to others. A man is "called" to an enterprise wider than the simple exploitation of "his own." He is not invited primarily to seek a maximum profit. The underlying premise is of a group of people some-how unified, a public with needs to be met and having "at its call" a number of persons of specified talents and interests. Men are, in a fashion appropriate to their talents, "called" by this public—both in the sense of being summoned and, originally, of being identified or named. Men are what they are called upon to do. Written records and the continuities of lineage no longer permit fresh labeling of "bakers," "smiths," "carpenters," "gardeners," "coopers," "wheelers," "millers." But men still are located, or "allocated," in that they are where they can do what society wants done.

Such an account of economic activity does not support an abstract or inalienable right to property—to do with one's own as one wishes. But it does contain the heart of the classic right to property. It provides that abilities are to be challenged and exercised in an activity to which they are suited; and the suita-bility of the activity must be congruent with the individual's beliefs about what he can do. He is free to follow such ordi-nary callings as he chooses. Yet such liberty necessarily looks beyond the individual. The community limits the range of the callings that are ordinary, as well as identifying those which are important to it.

The liberty to follow the ordinary callings certainly included the liberty to be a baker in New York in 1905, a ticket-seller (though not a fraudulent scalper) in New York City in 1927, a scrub-woman in Washington, D.C., in 1923. That liberty did not in the abstract consist of working for any given number of hours, or for any wage, or of selling one's wares on any terms that one might individually desire. For liberty there must in-deed be choice, and choice depends upon a certain balance of bargaining power. To restore the balance of economic power by state regulation is thus to restore the liberty to follow the calling in question. Government interference might, of course, be excessive and might improperly abridge the liberty of either employer or employee. Restriction of hours of work to 50 percent of the going community practice presumably would constitute such an abridgment. But such matters are the business of courts to decide. They do not fall under an absolute freedom of contract.

It is indeed the complexity of determining the proper conduct and character of economic callings that moved Walter Lippmann in *The Good Society* to hold that the market's division of labor alone should decide where when and how men should work. But the market system itself faces grave internal difficulties in the form of endemic inequalities of market power. In addition, many tasks must be carried out which are not just the satisfaction of individual needs. There are common concerns as well as those constituted by the adding together of individual interests. Indeed it is a matter of indifference, within quite wide limits, where men apply their energies; the decisive consideration is not merely a market criterion but their desire to have their work "mean something." They wish to feel that they are called upon to be useful.

The ordinary callings are those defined by public need and public order. They are as fixed or as fluid as the society is: typically, in our society they change rather rapidly in response to technological advances and developing consumer needs. New undertakings can establish themselves as ordinary callings in an industrial society that institutionalizes change. But there will be limits to the novelty, such as exclusion of piracy or murder, and such limits are practically set in official cases by government, specifically by the Courts.

To follow the ordinary callings is to conform with public order, that is, with due process of law. Government may intervene in this pursuit only as it, too, heeds the requirements of due process—as it treats men "equally" and otherwise adheres to established procedure. The public may intervene in any phase of economic activity—in hiring, firing, selling, buying, investing, working, joining unions, not joining unions —provided it observes accepted principles. In such intervention the public will be doing what smaller "publics"—firms, unions, other organizations—can and must do. The "busied man" cannot be "free" in the sense of "nonresponsible."

The Style of Public Intervention

The principle of public intervention was expressed with customary crispness by Rousseau: the Sovereign may concern itself only with what is of general importance, but the Sovereign must decide what is of general importance. The critical question is how the public may know when and how to intervene. The first, if negative, criterion is that intervention should be educational so far as possible. We assume, that is, that the economy has effective though not fully adequate elements of self-government in it and that these can be strengthened by information and suggestion. We assume that as a rule men will want to work usefully and will find a place to do it; we assume that others will pay them fairly for their work. We are committed to Adam Smith's belief in the merits of having one private interest contend against another. We accept competition as our ordinary economic mode, even though like Adam Smith we are concerned about the personal development of the makers of pins and pills and pencils. Our interventions, then, are conceived as devices to remove such "corruptions" as make fair competition impossible or prevent the capabilities of individuals from being exercised in socially significant activity. Normally we will intervene first by "educating"; we will coerce only as education fails.

The formula that government may and should intervene to supplement the forces of public opinion and of competition is not precise. It is pragmatic, essentially in the of Mr. Justice Holmes. Though his own economic sympathies were conservative, he was most impressive when voicing haughty and urbane reproof of efforts to sweep back the tides of the social regulation of business. He was confident, perhaps, that genuine economic liberty would survive any niggling state interference. Or perhaps his dominant concern was simply to maintain dignity under pressure, or to assure the due process of law in the widest sense. Certainly the social foundations he treasured were not to be shaken by such restraints on business as expressed the requirements of common morality.

The case for a moderate position is *de facto* supported presently by the fate of extreme theories. On the left the teachings of Marx and Lenin seem ever more undercut by Communist practice, even if this throws a somewhat more kindly light on their ultimate goals. On the right the competition of economic atoms seems hardly more useful as a model. We move uneasily from radical antimonopoly policies to those which find a soul in each corporation or labor union. The difficulties confronting the axioms of classical economics make plausible the contention that no exact formula is available and that Holmes's pragmatism is in this area our most promising theoretic basis.

The important problem for intervention is political. Galbraith's defense of "countervailence" expresses the declaration of Mr. Chief Justice Hughes in *Jones & Laughlin v. NLRB*[9] that bargaining power must be equalized. As Holmes might have put it, the fight must be fair.[10] Economic life is in part a fight. It is a form of activity in which the public good is to be served, up to a point, in a conflict of self-seekings. The public concern is that one man's liberty in following his calling does not abridge the liberty of another.

GOVERNMENT AS SPOKESMAN FOR THE ORDINARY CALLINGS

Government's ability to hold to a minimum its coercive intervention in the economy depends upon its effectiveness as public educator. The education is of adults, of mature participants in the economic struggle; the student body is no captive audience. The government is only one teacher among many; individuals and groups must be free to publish their own accounts of how the people fare as they pursue the ordinary callings. What kind of education, then, can government offer?

Government does, of course, already educate very broadly in this field. In the immense accumulation of factual data that streams from the Government Printing Office there is made available instrumental knowledge of great import about our production, our population, our income, our price level, our prospects. Such information is valuable to those in business and those who regulate business. The development of such data is indispensable to inform that intelligence corps demanded by Walter Lippmann in *Public Opinion*[11]—a group which could refine such data and formulate it so that it would be knowable by the public.

Such education must combine the authority of impartiality with the relevance appropriate to urgent controversy. As the economy is competitive, typically the need for public education is when competition becomes intractable. The kind of public education that meets this need was admirably set out in principle by Walter Lippmann in *Public Opinion* as he considered the merits of the Steel Strike of 1919. He argued for a hearing that really was open. He stipulated that the contending parties disclose their records to public scrutiny if they proposed to invoke public support. What a given party refused to reveal would be treated as irrelevant. Though such public education might not terminate the dispute, it would be in the long run more useful than a seizure of the property or capitulation by either party. The central problem was to generate an effective public opinion; relevant facts on wages, profits, standards of living, work rules, productivities, costs were literally to be "made public" so that the community as a whole might think reasonably on the issue.[12]

Intervention by government in such a hearing is a delicate affair: as one considers the play of political pressures upon such an investigation, it is hard to be sure that objectivity and *expertise* can be maintained rather than bent and twisted to serve partisan need. "Facts" are difficult to determine with accuracy; they involve predictions as well as histories. Private parties have their own fact-finders whose own vested interests hang on the reception accorded their findings. Intervention in any major dispute has political implications for persons and parties: presidents may be made by policemen's strikes or denied power because of plant seizures. The greater the power of public opinion, the greater the pressure it is under from special interests.

The role of government mediation typically goes beyond

hearing opposing sides in a dispute and subjecting their claims to public criticism. In such anguished industrial debates as those involving the loss of thousands of jobs through automation, government mediation must apply imagination and perspective to preserve the best of each opposing view without simply resorting to compromise. The art of such effective industrial statesmanship, already well established, requires constant renewal, and so does its presentation to the public. Perhaps our most familiar efforts at such public presentations are the presidential news conferences. These are fearfully subject to political considerations, but they can be an honest and fruitful source of public illumination. They can confirm genuine presidential leadership; they can inform an attentive public.

To ask that government take a leading role in developing the public intelligence about economic problems is to ask for more than "just facts." It is to ask also that government take part in formulating and asserting our national purposes. It is to provide for this, both in the context of urgent industrial strife and also in the long-run appraisal and planning of national resources in terms of national needs. It is to consider what our pattern of employment should be in decades to come. It is here that specialists in education may contribute from their experience in the development of persons and groups. The ordinary callings which are to direct our working talents are not simply a given cultural deposit confirmed in usage. The callings are, like the community they express, in process of development, and government has in virtue of its power and its range a singular perspective upon them. There is danger that government will be the great and only "caller" and that through its power it will dictate attitudes as well as choices of men; it has the greatest ability to pay the piper. Yet our only alternative is to permit our private information agencies to do the same thing in matters that affect the public as a whole.

Academic social scientists often have argued that government's role can and should be restricted to gathering facts. This view reflects a separation of social data from social principles; pursuant to this conception the controversial exploration of principles should be left to private, usually academic, agencies. "Let government do the research in an unbiased way," runs the argument, "and leave to individuals and groups the thinking, the advocacy." But a social science so conceived is academic and sterile. Its concepts are "empty," its data "blind." Or, since empty concepts really cannot function at all, such science reflects perforce the most conventional and unobtrusive of concepts. The development of a social science which pursues facts in a framework of significant principle is as yet more of a dream than a reality. Yet it is the only hope for a knowledge in which a community's hopes for itself can be known and tested. If government is to seek facts government must concern itself with principles.

The task of educating the public and the public's business involves special gifts of imagination and invention. It goes far beyond merely holding up the mirror. We have developed a special agent for this process in the "public relations officer," and we find him at once our hope and our despair. We choose for the job a man decent and likeable. But his decency is often an instrument of manipulation. He seems dedicated to the indiscriminate "relating" of a group to the public, as one might to an elephant who happened to be in the house: peanuts and other pacifiers must be provided. Not all public relations officers follow the lead of the real estate lobbyist in Washington who was quoted as describing democracy as "stinking."[13] But in much public relations work there is an element of externality which identifies the public as some sort of great beast. When a public relations officer declares an interest, the public is bound to suspect a special bias is at work. In public relations the confounding of business and education reaches genuine confusion. Like the ancient Sophist, the public relations officer is handicapped by the fact that his teaching is for hire.

The lesson cannot be, however, to stop trying to establish proper understanding by the public. We must, rather, widen and deepen exchange of essential information about publicly important matters so that shoddy, deceitful representations are readily identified. The public meanings of government's actions and the actions of private parties must be clarified so that the public can see and judge for itself. In our corrupted "public relations" such meanings are systematically obscured lest the status of a client be impaired. A true public relations officer expresses a more enduring confidence in those he serves. Rather, he expresses confidence in those under whose authority he speaks; for he is, indeed, intermediary between the public which is judging and the public which is judged. He must develop so far as he can the intellectual quality of our academic institutions at their best.

GOVERNMENT EDUCATION BY GOVERNMENT DEED

As we conclude this review of government as public instructor, we need to keep in mind that government educates most effectively by example. Our most urgent domestic questions presently center about racial discrimination and the confusion of our uneasy cities. In both of these all our governments have important roles to play. Federal examples of equal treatment, in the armed forces and in public employment, are obvious stimuli to antidiscrimination efforts. So is the federal undertaking to help in the effort to renew or redevelop or redesign our metropolitan complexes. Such federal undertakings do not commit us to centering all urban planning in Washington. But local and private moneys and plans are not by themselves adequate to meet our cities' problems. To supply information and material encouragement is at once educational and economic in impact. It is to convey with experience the lesson of what can be done with given resources in a given situation. It is to provide concrete assurance that such efforts can be part of a coherent national effort.

One of the most important educational implications of such an effort is to be associated with its effect upon professional social scientists and the public's attitude toward them. The economic analysis and reporting suggested here are not restricted to conventional price analysis. It may hope to draw on that analysis for theoretic rigor. But it also will hope to bring the "pure economist" into rapport with the other social sciences and the humanities and also to bridge the gap between business and the schools. Essentially the proposed studies will try to see how men's work is related to the entire community life, to determine how managing and working are significant for self-government. Such a Public Economics will require, in proportion to its effectiveness, the full support of the academic community if it is to resist political pressures.

Some social scientists, of course, raise the problem of public interest and of the public's capacity for broad education; some social scientists elevate apathy to a positive good. In so doing they conclude too easily that serious political interest cannot be reflective. We have far to go to achieve that condition, affirmed by Themistocles of the Athenians, in which the second thought is the same as the first. But only extended experience with serious public affairs can move us in that direction. And only such experience can help us manage the mountain of reporting that already overwhelms us as "required reading." In contrast with the bulk of details, the useful amount of public knowledge on vital matters is sadly slight. The leverage of public sponsorship is indispensable if the right knowledge is to be made available to the public.

Government as School Board for the Country

The suggestion that American businessmen assume, under federal auspices, a formal role in the direction of American education may seem to Americans more shocking than Plato's proposal of philosopher-rulers. Academia may seem therewith betrayed to its two most formidable enemies. For while boards of trustees and local school boards sometimes have achieved high distinction in associating business representatives with the educational process, still, as Middletown's history has shown us, the conceptions of education held by such boards often are uninspired. For the country as a whole it hardly can be said that businessmen have regarded this function as calling for the application of energies of the same order as those applied in business. School board work is for after hours, a generous contribution to community needs. On the other

hand, academic persons have been reluctant to see businessmen "too interested" in the schools.

Yet American education is today tremendously big business.
It involves an immense investment in equipment and machinery. It is all-inclusive in its "raw materials"—all children
and many adults, too. It aims at end products deemed desirable—voters, bachelors, masters, doctors. There are real simi-
larities between factories and schools, and on these men
experienced in business can have much to say. If schools
shape human material in one way, work in factory and field
shapes it also, though such influence is not presently an
object of concern—except peripherally—to those who manage
our economy.

Our pattern of population growth means massive new educational construction as well as the founding of new institutions, and in such enterprises the counsel of the businessman
is essential. He will offer this in association with local agencies
so far as their financial powers suffice. But federal money also
must be invested heavily, and it is in that spending that we
need the best advice we can muster on the proper allocation
of resources. It is quite intelligible to conceive our education,
in the reflective sense, as our most prized investment.

There must be in the federal government a really effective
board for planning the broad outlines of our national education enterprise. Such a board must include persons from business and labor as well as law and other professions. This
would be, despite Mr. Justice Frankfurter's warning, a "school
board for the country."[14] Better, it would be the school boards'
school board—an enlargement of our present Office of Education. It would not conduct centralized surveillance of
every textbook and teaching procedure; indeed, it could contain and temper such assaults from local groups. It would
declare very broad policy and judge its fulfilment. A national
school board must be a group of citizens, representative of
the whole community, charged with the selection of those
administrative officials who have the appropriate wits and
funds to see that the best teachers are found. Such a board
must know enough about both teaching and administration to

be able to appraise the administrators. The guarantee of academic freedom is not absence of community concern. It is rather assurance that teachers will be chosen and rewarded in terms of their discharge of their proper public function. A proper school board maintains its teachers in the style suitable to their special calling. And in the definition of that style it assures a full hearing to the teachers as well as to other functional groups.

Mr. Justice Frankfurter's attack on the notion of the Supreme Court as national school board was not expressly disputed by his associates, even though in the second flag salute case[15] they rejected his stand on the compulsory flag salute, as well as his appeal to judicial self-restraint. The Supreme Court's majority did not, in their "libertarian activism," argue for detailed inspection by the Court of our educational practices. They did not challenge our tradition of day-by-day control by local authorities. But they did announce that the federal principle affirmed in the First Amendment is to be interpreted to protect freedom of thought and religion in the public schools; and similar decisions have been handed down in cases involving school bus fares,[16] released time,[17] the recital of prayers in school,[18] and the reading of the Bible.[19] In such decisions the principle of the national review of educational practices is explicitly established.

Although American schools have been "publicly owned" in the main, their local character has made them, in national terms, less than fully public. They have thus been denied the resources which only the national community can supply. As we turn now, belatedly, to make such resources available, we shall need the best counsel of men trained and successful in the major operations of industry and trade—men whose talents are the counterpart of that intellectual equipment which can promote public enlightenment about our business activity. The men who have served with distinction as trustees of private institutions need to become trustees for the nation's education as a whole—to bring their practical wisdom to bear on employing American money to develop American minds.

There is a revealing and rather touching account of a businessman's interest in education in Woodrow Wilson's essay, *When A Man Comes to Himself*, written in 1901, a short time before Wilson became president of Princeton. In a clear though not express reference to Andrew Carnegie, who was to become Wilson's friend and admirer, Wilson wrote fervently of the personal fulfilment of a business leader who, having made a fortune, discovered his full powers in bestowing his money on a project such as a university. The notable Institute at which these lectures were delivered and the Carnegie Foundation are among the many fitting memorials to Mr. Carnegie's generosity. But they do not—nor did Wilson's essay—offer evidence that Carnegie's mind was really active in relation to education. Carnegie did not, it seems, push his thinking about education beyond planning to continue his own education sometime in the future. He could well have "come to himself" more fully had he been able, in a manner less external than giving a lake to Princeton, to participate seriously in its long-range policies. There were trustees on the Princeton board, both friends and foes of Wilson, who did enter actively into Princeton's government. The intensity of their participation no doubt reflected Wilson's own passionate concern, just as the controversy over Wilson's policies showed how much such business trustees might differ among themselves.

A Businesslike National Education Policy

Businessmen rarely applaud higher taxes. But the argument for increasing the 3½ percent of our gross national product that now goes to education may be formulated in economic terms quite appealing to a business-minded federal school board. Increased "input" will yield increased "output" in the form of greater responsiveness to community summons. On the negative side it will reduce the taxes needed for relief. Schools will develop more fully the skills demanded by our complex economy, including the flexibility which a changing economy requires. The perspectives of workers will be enlarged so as to let them choose more rationally where they will work, what jobs they will perform, and how they will spend their time and money. More education will help our economy to remain individualistic by making more secure the opportunity for rational choice.

There is little validity in the objection that the economy cannot accommodate all the products of a generously financed school system. If it is folly to develop a skill one can never use, it is more foolish still to let lie fallow men's capacities for adaptation and development. There is a state better than that of either frustrated Sophists' pupil or satisfied fool. Men can be educated broadly and with special stress on preparing for a world in which most business consists of serving people rather than handling materials or machines. Such flexible education is, indeed, often recommended by business and law schools as the best preparation for an active career. A government which permits its educated people to become pathologically demoralized from unemployment has failed in its relation to business rather than in its educational policies.

Achievement of maximum national productivity is an intelligible and important objective. But production of consumer goods is only one component in that comprehensive aim which is men's attaining the full reach of their powers. Such a conception moves business thinking on to those wider horizons in which education is seen as essentially the nurture of human qualities. It affects men's value to one another, as well as to themselves; it makes them mutually committed to a life of ordered liberty. We cannot reckon the winning of the highest return on our educational dollars on a strict accounting scale. A broadened national education may well involve a considerable redistribution of wealth, enlarging the academic share at the expense of the rest. But the issue should be both a larger total product to distribute and—more important—a product richer in intrinsic satisfactions.

The formula for our educational spending can be based upon the performances of our best schools—defining "best" as those on which there is substantial consensus among college admissions officers. In the considerable number of such schools we see children genuinely grow and flower, in contrast with their fate in those less happy institutions where they creep grumbling along like snails. Our new spending can be directed by indices of child development rather than being devoted dominantly to accumulating the shiny aids of audio-visual equipment and closed television circuits. This is not to disparage the continuing search for better ways to teach. But we have inherited enduringly valid standards, in contrast with which much of the new educational "science" is analogous to new fender styles in automobiles. New ventures generally seem desirable more for their novelty than for the character of the gadget introduced. They are significant as they are employed by teachers who can retain responsiveness to freshness and novelty; who, above all, can stimulate activity.

THE PERILS OF POLITICS IN EDUCATION

The national school board is to encourage throughout the schools the best teaching practices it can find. It will face the traditional liberal fear of federal control. It will be reminded of the failures of traditional and ritualistic inductions into official Americanism. It will hear once more John Stuart Mill's solemn reminder that a nation that dwarfs its men can accomplish nothing great.

The standard civics course probably has prompted more un-American reactions than could ever be blamed on the teachings of Karl Marx. Such courses have seemed devised as by some invisible hand to show our public in a guise utterly at odds with any healthy private interests. But the public background of citizenship need not assume such dull colors. It is easy to conceive how in any given school the local politics and history might be shown in continuity with the larger American scene. Some texts already dip into the rich storehouse of America's past. The labors, boredom, fears, triumphs, excitements, humor, bitterness of the American enterprise—the mixtures of small purposes and great ones— these are the stuff from which American citizenship has been made, and these can be communicated to the young. Above all, American political life can and must be shown as a series

of real choices in real controversies. This requires a high
order of teaching talent, for the teachers must really know
the material and still manage it in ways suitable to effective
teaching. The development of such teachers is the price we
pay for educating the youth to be at once patriotic and interesting. It is the price long since recommended by Jefferson,
despite his trust in the intuitive virtue of men who live on the
land.

A second criticism of extending federal aid and federal
influence is that they will tend to drive thoughtful, independent teachers out of the schools. The presently governing
Supreme Court decision on government policy toward "subversive teachers" is *Adler v. Board of Education*. There the
Court upheld New York State's Feinberg Law which excludes from public school teaching those who are members
of organizations on a proscribed list drawn up by the State
University Regents. It is true that the character of the membership and the list of organizations are to be examined with
all due process of law. And in the law's enforcement efforts
have been made to follow procedures academically accept-
able. Yet through the *Adler* decision it has been made official
policy to judge teachers by political tests: "from time im-
memorial," Mr. Justice Minton said, "a teacher is known by
the company he keeps." Association is decisive, whether with
Communists or publicans or sinners. The school is where
young minds are formed, Minton argued, and so the state
must see that the schools are politically pure.

It is the prospect of such reasoning in a federally sponsored
education system that sets many teachers and friends of
teachers against any extension of federal spending on education. Yet the alternative is more dangerous. It leaves education
to be expanded by local units unable to resist partisan pressures. It ignores the nationwide organization and financing of
groups which now try to impose political conformity on the
schools. It forgets that effective defenses of academic freedom
normally are conducted by national organizations of teachers.

The tragic defect in Mr. Justice Minton's reasoning is its
transposition of a local community moralism to the public

education of a modern nation-state. His argument is to be met, not by retreating to the local community, but by showing as Mr. Justice Black and Mr. Justice Douglas did in dissent that it is precisely for the sake of the national community that political tests must not be imposed. They wrote:

> A school system producing students trained as robots threatens to rob a generation of the versatility that is perhaps our greatest distinction. The Framers knew the dangers of dogmatism; they also knew the strength that comes when the mind is free, when ideas may be pursued wherever they lead.[20]

Their argument is public in concern as is that of the Court; the Court's error is in its blindness to what a truly strong and educated public is and what kinds of teachers it needs. But this blindness may itself yield to education that reveals the authentic sources of public strength. As we educate our governors more fully they will come to see more clearly why education must be judged in its own terms.

Finally it is a fact that federal money already is going in tremendous volume to universities and colleges, especially in programs devoted to science. There is little evidence that this has been attended by political interference. There must doubtless be eternal vigilance on the academic side, but a well-nourished academy is the better able to stay awake.

The Special Educational Problems

There are many particular problems which will attend heightened federal interest and influence. If a federal school board embodies a benevolent neutrality and an enthusiasm for education in general, it will become the object of all the partisan pressures that now hedge the schools around. The variety and strength of these in a city setting is well depicted in *Middletown in Transition* where the citizens' deep concern for their children's development was contrasted with their uncertainty how far to lean in this direction or that. On the national scale we have to achieve impartiality in controversies that involve religion and race and the basic frame of the cur-

riculum. We will have to spend more money without magnify-
ing our difficulties in like measure.

The crucial need is to deal with the special pressures in
terms of the public interest. It is my "Hamiltonian belief" that
this can be facilitated if our national educational policy
makers include men who have experienced success in business
enterprise, including the leadership of unions. Such men will
have a view of the importance of a coherent and efficient
enterprise broadly conceived to meet public needs. They
should be able to identify and discount the special representations of special groups. They may avoid solution by piecemeal
compromise. In such a group men of different creeds and
colors and constitutional theories may exemplify that effort
at unity in diversity which is the distinctive American undertaking.

Religion in the Public Schools

The problem of religion in the schools, in a nation committed as America is to religious freedom, will not be solved
to everyone's satisfaction. There is deep disagreement, under-
standably, on precisely what belongs to Caesar. There is
equally deep disagreement about exactly what "religion" is
and when we are acting "religiously." Such difficulties make
the prudent pluralist disposed to refrain from precise commitment. But we cannot avoid taking a stand; to do nothing
is still to act. Either the public will be effectively represented
through its government or special interests will exploit the
public machinery.

We may take some consolation from the fact that the more
urgent such private pressures the more urgent, too, the need
for finding the common ground which can support a public
stand. It is true that sectarian disagreements have recurrently
in recent years kept the Congress from acting with respect to
financial aid to schools and colleges. But we have been slowly
discovering our mind as to what we can and should do.

We have agreed, thus, that we will do much in assisting
public education even if we are at the same time making

easier the efforts of religious groups. In *Pierce v. Society of Sisters*[21] in 1925 we declared our willingness to accept private and sectarian schools as fulfilling the common educational requirements of the community. In other cases, notably the *Everson* bus fares case, we have justified spending public money in ways that ease the burden which a religious group otherwise might feel obliged to assume. We have been trying to provide, in such "child benefit" cases, those expenditures and services which any child or group in the community might reasonably claim. These certainly include police and fire protection, and presumably transportation and free lunches and some essential health services. Such a list probably should be extended. There still is need of much discretion, as there may be cases where existence of a sectarian school system would impose special burdens on the public budget; again there may be cases where, on a temporary basis and to assure adequate education, sectarian schools should be directly assisted. But it surely is the sense of the Constitution that public money and authority are not to serve religious purposes. They are neither to promote all religion—nor a particular religion—nor to discourage it. The morality which our political unity expresses is in itself independent of religion.

The reaction to the Supreme Court decision in the New York Regents' school prayer case, *Engel v. Vitale*[22] in 1962, showed both the general and partial motives at work. Extreme critics of the Court's outlawing of such prayers announced that the Court has "taken Christ out of the schools and put the Negroes in." More thoughtful supporters of the prayer doubtless believe that in heightening religious awareness they are serving a vital political purpose. The Court's lone dissenter, indeed, Mr. Justice Stewart, insisted that a voluntary prayer was only part of a free exercise of religion, and that such exercise has been part of public ceremonial in the United States since 1787. But the majority held, and plausibly, that whatever the case with other ceremonials, the reciting of such a school prayer does involve a step in establishing religion. A prayer, like the reading from a particular "Bible" or "translation of a Bible," necessarily expresses a particular conception of religion, of men's relation to the world and one another, and of the church to the state. Public means should be devoted only to public ends. And no one believes that the American public is, as a political entity, identical with any particular religious group. It may be that religious purposes are "higher" than those served by political organization. Similar claims may be made for esthetic values. But such priorities do not in themselves provide a basis for intervention in politics. From the public's point of view any religious group is private and as such entitled only to just and friendly treatment by the government.

The opinion by Mr. Justice McReynolds in *Pierce v. Society of Sisters* is tantalizing in its imprecision. "The child is not the creature of the state," he wrote; "those who nurture him and direct his destiny have the right, coupled with the high duty, to recognize and prepare him for additional obligations." The negative assertion no doubt is valid and so is the general prescription that the political order should be presented to school children as a set of institutions open to criticism. But the "additional obligations" cannot be in any simple sense affirmation of "religion." That men have been and are religious, that there is a religious conception of man and of nature, that men have agreed and also disagreed about the "truths" of religion—all these, in appropriate historic setting, should be introduced to the young. But, as Madison wrote to Jefferson when the Virginia Act of Religious Freedom was passed, our interest must be to "extinguish forever the ambitious hope of making laws for the human mind."[23] The kind of public unity we require is the kind that comes from minds making their own laws. This may be in terms of the mind's sense of its "additional obligations," but not as these are affirmed in the items that recently have been involved in controversy—the exploitation of school requirements in connection with "released time," the required or optional prayers, the Bible readings. These have been clearly the efforts of particular religious groups to influence the child. They have been, though in no impressive dimension, efforts to "make laws for the human mind" instead of preparing that mind to know and reflect upon its wider obligations.

RACIAL EQUALITY IN THE SCHOOLS

Our official public position is clear on the problem of racial distinctions in the schools, but our political difficulties are great. Here, as in the case of religion, the public agencies cannot be inactive. They are bound to work for that equality which is the cement of a self-governing public. They must find ways to promote desegregation, as by aiding schools which advance its cause and denying aid to those which do not. But the task is particularly one of effective education, of supplying the mediating devices that will bring whites and Negroes together in consultation. It must find ways to formulate educational policy in terms independent of race, terms that are properly considered, such as the child's residence and tastes and abilities.

Increased public spending on schools will draw money from the richer states, dominantly in the North, to the poorer southern states. The rich may resent this, but in fact the policy protects them against over-rapid influx of the poorly educated. Since 1954, indeed, the problem of race in education has become more clearly, year by year, a national problem. A century after the Emancipation Proclamation was signed, we have little to show in the way of a nationally supported education in which alone an enduring emancipation can be achieved.

Somewhat curiously, it is the conservative who is today the least enthusiastic for energetic pursuit of desegregation, while the liberals of the New Deal tradition are for it. I do not think that this upsets the analysis here offered of conservatives and liberals, any more than conventional political antitheses are upset by the fact that conservative Republicans seem bent on wooing the anti-Negro vote while the Democrats now court the Negro. The conservative, secure in his identification of Public Virtue, and of the distinct levels of men in terms of their grasp of that Virtue, is reluctant to change the order of human relationships by political interference. This conservative antipathy to politically induced change extends to such decisions of the courts as the conservative considers arbitrary. On the other side, liberal scepticism about the superior moral code of the conservative elect conduces to sympathy for egalitarian measures, even if with continuing bad conscience about the introduction of political authority.

Neither of these views clearly states the responsibility of our political authority to bring about that equality which is inherent in American self-government. The equality which implies a feeling of common citizenship is, as Mill said, an essential prerequisite of liberty. But that equality need not be the community barracks fellowship of the kibbutz or the Platonic rulers. Equality defined in political terms is not wholesale or "undiscriminating." The equality which government must promote is that equality of privileges and immunities which long have been stipulated in the Fourteenth Amendment. The equality we need to support in education is that equality, not a wholesale "social amalgamation."

The liberal is on firm ground when he speaks against "legislating preferences," but in dealing with education we are necessarily arranging behaviors in a manner which affects minds and characters. Desegregation may be expected, as it brings about association from the earliest school years, to reduce the importance of skin color in the minds of white and colored children alike. But the effort will succeed only when the negative effort to eliminate discrimination can be given up in favor of positive concentration in absorbing educational enterprises which focus common attention. The only equality which will be persuasive and enduring will be that of genuinely common activity. This will not deny authentic differentials of ability; it need not threaten the hard-won social position of those lately arrived minority groups who tend to be among the bitter enemies of school desegregation. It will be an equality of opportunity and of common standards, in which respect for persons coexists with recognition of differences.

WHAT SHALL WE TEACH?

Extensive federal spending on education can promote the sense of generality, not only in the context of religious and racial contentions, but also in respect of the materials and disciplines handled in the schools. Such an influence, though not so spectacular, probably is the most permanently significant to the development of our schools and colleges. Up to now, indeed, government assistance has been uneven.

Our principal programs of aid to date have been in scientific research and the training of scientists. We have been willing, as in the National Defense Education Act, to assimilate to "science" projects which fall under the languages and the social sciences. Probably the flexibility of the programs will continue in the direction of including all academic disciplines in the areas to be assisted. But at present the conception of "related to the national interest" is both cloudy and somewhat suspect; it requires the arts of educational salesmanship to extend it beyond the more narrow coverages of military defense.

The "affluent professor" or research operator and the fund-raising college president are in some sense necessary links between the academy and the federal school board. Someone must carry the initial argument as to why money should be spent here rather than there. But the process must transcend the mentality of the market place. Financial aid must be determined, not just in relation to science or to the cold war, but to the humane and progressive development of a national community. Policy at present is far too directly pressed to "show results."

The proper function of federal aid is really to give the academic community its chance. We need to become generous with open-end grants to students and teachers as the academy sees fit. We need to make it possible for the serious educator, as well as the "operator," to be persuasive with the federal school board. It is only by showing such confidence in education that the control of science in terms of the humanities and social sciences can be brought about. Only thus can our ritual pieties about the values of philosophic and esthetic reflection be made meaningful. This is not to impose a particular philosophy or esthetic or a special view of the relation of science to the public. It is rather to hold that the scientist's busy explorations of causes and conditions shall fall into place in human activity generally. It is to locate the right ordering of such studies in the hands of academic persons who will be assured of adequate facilities for the job. If this can be done, the public import of science as instrument of common need and refiner of common reflection may be saved from that corruption in which it devises ingenious gadgets to enrich our own consumption or to help us annihilate other people.

The position taken here may once again be contrasted with the conservative and liberal views introduced in the preceding chapter. The conservative holds that a complete and substantive code of ethics should inform and control government; the liberal assigns such authority only to the private interests or ideals of individuals or groups. The liberal takes his cue from economic activity, as conceived in the classic free enterprise tradition, while the conservative inspiration is essentially educational. The liberal is impressed with the importance of adult men freely seeking their fortunes, according to their own judgment; the conservative sees men's need for guidance and improvement by those who think more clearly and at longer range.

Clearly there is much truth in each of these positions, but both are deficient in failing to acknowledge the fact of equal dealing among adult and responsible persons. They share the belief that there is little hope for genuine mutuality when men in general propose to cooperate. This is why, as I see it, these doctrines have helped to keep American business and education out of right relation with one another—why they have suffered from mutual disrespect and from overt failure to support one another. We have been sometimes excessively conservative in imposing community standards in defiance of academic freedom and sometimes excessively liberal in allowing the schools to go their own way or in refusing to the nation's business the criticism and instruction it needs. We have not identified those areas in our economic life—the adjustment of men's talents to their proper callings—which educators are qualified to judge; and we have not brought to the planning of education that independence and hardheadedness which at best characterize the American entrepreneur.

We have not formulated clearly the continuities between government and business and the schools. Government, formally, is the management of official relations among men; business formally deals with the producing and managing of goods, things useful to men; education formally deals with human development. We have failed, in considering the relations among these, to recognize the legitimate, indeed the necessary, role of government in appraisal and appointment of teaching. Government should not concern itself with technology, in business or teaching. But government is commissioned in a free society to promote the right human activities and to restrict these, too, within the appropriate social limits. Government needs to be sufficiently businesslike, sufficiently cultivated, to know how to be active and how to restrain its activity in relation to the people's business and the people's schools.

We have here the basis on which to appraise John Dewey's account of education in relation to the public. Though Dewey supported the conservative stress on men's capacity to be improved by proper instruction, he emphasized still more the dangers in imposing upon the young the standards of the older generation. He took his stand, effectively, as leader of the liberals as he proclaimed the now battered doctrines of progressive education.

I believe that John Dewey's failure to win a more enduring influence reflects his unwillingness to concede the possibility of a common language holding together the old and young, the established and the new. He stressed the sheer external impositions which are, certainly, real enough in human experience. But he was not ready to recognize the form of discourse in which human beings, disagreeing, still can manage that disagreement so as to remove it from the realm of raw conflict. That the young must "adjust" to the established world

IV

Responsible Government—The Freedom
of Public Discussion

THE GOVERNMENT of a free society is not only a popular government which reveals and informs those common purposes which are as real as the purposes of individuals and private groups. It is not only an active government which defines and carries out our fundamental public intentions in managing our resources and training our minds and characters. A government which is the instrument and expression of freedom must respond to, indeed must foster, the searching and unrestricted discussion of all public affairs. To say this is, once more, to recite our ancient faith—or possibly to parade our deepest illusion. As we consider the freedom of public discussion, we must review our currently beguiling folklores to determine how far we may affirm this, our most fundamental creed.

One of our most emphatic prophets of scepticism was a fellow traveler of the Founders; in *Common Sense* Thomas Paine proclaimed a distinction which has remained persuasive to many Americans:

> Some writers have so far confounded society with government, as to leave little or no distinction between them; whereas, they are not only different, but have different origins. Society is produced by our wants and government by our wickedness; the former promotes our happiness positively by uniting our affections, the latter negatively by restraining our vices. The one encourages intercourse, the other creates distinctions. The first is a patron, the last a punisher. Society in every state is a blessing but government, even in the best state, is but a necessary evil.[1]

101

On Paine's account society is men associating voluntarily whereas government involves compulsion. Social man is free; governed man is not. So held an early strain of that political theory which Walter Lippmann has labeled "dangerous Jacobinism."[2]

The account which I have offered of government's relation to our associated economic and educational activities has been intended to formulate precisely the continuity between society and government which Paine denied. Amiable and cooperative human interchange, in which we are truly "social," is necessarily the concern of government. On the other hand, the restraint of men's antisocial propensities is *de facto* the mission of all our nongovernmental associations, from the corporations that hire and pay according to work done to the schools that certify the talents and achievements of the workers to be. Both society and government may be, at given times, necessary evils: both impose burdens we would gladly leave to others. But both offer on the other side opportunities for the larger and more expansive career. In both freedom can be found, though in both it is hard to find.

This is not to say that social and political activity are one and the same. But each makes its positive moral contribution to the life of the public. Government is to be identified as much with the public education it can foster as with the prisons it must maintain, just as prisons must be more than institutions merely for detention or retribution.

The procedure that makes the difference between free association and forced association is communication among those who associate. A free society's hallmark is the transformation of externally imposed common activity into programs which are commonly understood and, so far as possible, commonly supported. This does not mean that "the people will be taught to be unanimous," for discussion characteristically opens divisions as much as it closes them. But divisions discussed can be intelligible and tolerable. As Theodore White remarks in his analysis of the 1960 presidential election, even the closest result will be accepted by Americans so long as the processes of free debate and free voting have been as-sured.[3]

The public discussion is what constitutes the public. Stop the talk, or the potential talk, and the public ceases to be. It is only by recognizing this that political theory finds a proper course between the assertion of a doubtless illusory "Real Will" and retreat into moral individualism. Thoughts can be shared, as feelings can be shared, and loyalties, too. But such sharing is a work of art, of human effort, as much as it is a product of nature. Natural affections may be, as Rousseau said, the necessary materials for a sense of community. But in themselves they are not distinctively moral. They achieve the universality requisite for moral quality only as they are associated in the intentions which animate common activity.

The self-governing community is distinguished by the active and lively sense of government's close relation with the com-mon purposes of persons in the community.[4] And this means that public discussion is at once the clarifier and the creator of public purposes. Those who, like the Callers to Public Virtue, insist that only virtuous discussion should be permitted miss the point that public discussion *is* virtue in the public domain. It is the offering of ideas for general approval and general adoption. It is committing oneself to judgment by one's neighbor. It is announcing one's willingness to act on the common public stage. He who declares his views on public policy affirms in his own way, however modest, that same conviction of relevance which a candidate affirms as he runs for office, high or lowly.

The relation between public discussion and government is necessarily complex. It is clear that a government which is popular is incessantly discussed. It will not frequently be praised, but it will never be ignored. It must be critically and unmercifully examined. It must be internally so constituted that it can examine itself as well as expose itself to critical survey from outside.

But government also, from its side, defines and prescribes the range of discussion of public affairs, and it is in this area that our immediate policy tensions have appeared. The diverse and mighty reach of modern government makes inevitable its participation in the great process of assertion and counter-assertion. Government must help to make clear, by factual research and by analysis of principle, what our national intentions are. Government must inquire to what extent the privately owned agencies of discussion are adequate to their task.[5] And government will no doubt be prepared to institute, over and above the official educational institutions, such other sources of study and publicity as are required to maintain the public discussion in its task of building a moral public. The role of government is as much to get out the relevant expressions of opinion as it is to impose restrictions on those behaviors which profess to be discussion but are not. Government must encourage, protect, promote to the full *public* speech—that is, speech for or about or by the public.

The status of public discussion in a democracy is clearly presented against the background of majority rule. That "the majority should conclude all the rest" is, except as other arrangements are explicitly made, practically an absolute for democratic politics. It also has been a source of anxiety since the Republic began. Currently consciousness is high of the insecurity of minorities—of wealth or creed or color. And the Federalist Paper Ten prescriptions for mitigating the dangers of majority tyranny hardly seem to apply today. Yet majority rule within the context of genuinely free public discussion appears tolerable and indeed essentially connected with self-government.

The crucial role of the public discussion is to make the majority justify itself. The majority must show itself the best approximation that can be mustered for the general will. To remind the gentlemen of the majority that they may be mistaken, that they are not a law unto themselves, that they have to speak for the whole community, past, present, and future, is to make tolerable the situation of the minority. It is to change its condition from one of numbers alone to one of numbers argued and reasoned. It is to promise, absolutely, that the present majority must again face in regular season the challenge of the popular choice. The public discussion is the practical guarantee of the society's control of its government.

The Meaning of the First Amendment

We may give these statements concrete reference through attention to the urgent practical problem which has confronted us in the past half-century. Responding to fears for our national security and the preservation of our own institutions, we have been struggling to interpret fairly the uncompromising language of the First Amendment, that Congress shall make no law abridging the freedom of speech. The positions taken, within and outside the Supreme Court, have ranged from saying that the amendment means exactly what it seems to say to holding that such freedom must give way when other pressing needs are to be met. The tangled web of the argument shows that we still are far, as a community, from having formulated fully clear meanings for "abridging" and "freedom" and "speech." We move toward clarity, I believe, if we consider directly the public office and import of free discussion.

The public, through its government, of course imposes many restrictions on utterance, and in areas close to those which the libertarian holds most dear. In the academy we restrict men's words about as much as we protect and promote them. We assume that in our schools teachers must be held to account for what they say. They are hired, fired, rewarded in terms of their words. Their words must not be "improperly" restricted, but they must be limited—in the teaching function —to such as are suitable in the training of the young. The teacher speaks within the context of educational purposes which define his freedom. This is not to say that he must not be "controversial" or that he may not hold unpopular views; but he must speak with relevance and in a manner which the academic authorities declare to be fitting for a teacher. He can be free only insofar as he fulfils his public responsibility.[6]

In the economic market place, again, for all our enthusiasm

for free expression, we do not apply the First Amendment's protections to the advertising that supports our daily press and radio and television. A cynic may comment that such speech may invoke protectors mightier than the First Amendment. But the principled basis of our attitude toward advertising is that it so clearly expresses a private interest. It offers no serious public claim. It announces a private undertaking to meet—and normally also to arouse—a private need.

The converse of this is government's power to compel disclosure in the public interest. Of corporations, unions, lobbyists, and others serving private purposes, government does and must on occasion require participation in the great public discussion, on the ground that this is essential in assuring self-government in the society at large. We have not decided in full detail where compulsory disclosure can reach; but there is no doubt that we accept it as consistent with our belief in the public freedom of speech.

On the other hand, we do insist on a hearing for utterances which genuinely concern the public, even if such utterances are heavy with private purposes as well. A classic example is provided by Mr. Justice Murphy's opinion in the case of *Thornhill v. Alabama*.[7] There Murphy, following the lead of Mr. Justice Brandeis in the *Senn* case,[8] declared peaceful picketing to be under the First Amendment shield. It is understood that picketing is not always peaceful and that pickets speak in terms of grievance. But the force of the Brandeis-Murphy criterion is that the picketing communication is indispensable in the formation of the representative public opinion. The *Thornhill* decision was not for Thornhill's sake or that of his fellows on the picket line. Rather it was for Alabama and the integrity of Alabama's deliberation on a labor dispute. The freedom of speech is identified expressly in terms of its public import. It is the freedom a public decision has in virtue of public discussion. It is the freedom a public may have of doing what it thinks it should do. Speech by employees, employers, or any "interested" parties must be given its chance to contribute to a public attitude on matters in which the public is interested.

Public speech must be unrestricted because it is the condition of the public's freedom: it is what throws light on public affairs and what is aimed to influence the public's actions. Such speech—in contrast with libelous or riotous speech or advertising, which serve private purposes—is essential to instruct the public action and keep the public in being. Public discussion develops the common purposes and activity which transform a collection of private persons into an effective public. To be free we must know the truth and, as well, act upon it together.

The Heritage of John Stuart Mill

My argument inevitably retraces, but in some measure departs from, the reasoning of the great guiding saint of modern liberals, John Stuart Mill. To Mill's warm hospitality toward men and thoughts unusual and individual we owe a never-ending debt. So do we, too, for his defense of radically free discussion.[9] But Mill was not as cogent in his argument as he was plausible in his conclusions. The weakness in his reasoning has persisted to cloud our present thinking.

Mill argued in the first chapter of *On Liberty* that thought and discussion must be free because they fall within that sphere where individuals harm others only insofar as those others freely chose to be harmed. Speech is a man's own business, and others need not concern themselves with it if they decide to ignore him. But in his second chapter Mill contended that discussion must be free because of its utility to that truth which society needs. Thus Mill held first that speech need not upset society, but second that speech is indispensable to society. In fact, as is shown in his references to Jesus and Socrates, he accepted and welcomed precisely the kinds of speech which society finds most "upsetting."

Finding fallacies in *On Liberty* and *Utilitarianism* has been an academic pastime ever since Mill wrote them; no doubt it will continue as long as they are read. And Mill will be read by liberals, surely, as long as men have liberty to read at all. We need to recast his first argument—to "remove" the freedom of discussion from its "location" in an "individual" sphere where a man is "on his own," not bothering other men. We need to understand that when a man is speaking his own mind others have an obligation to listen. We need also to clarify Mill's second argument in its account of the utility of thought and discussion: we need to say that some speech is the medium through which individuals cease to be islands to themselves. We need to make explicit the humane and rational quality which discussion confers upon actions. We must recognize in the speech that is general in scope and reference the building of a genuine public, a human order in which men's horizons are broadened to take on moral character. In his formal statement (though not in its practical effect) Mill ignored what Rousseau set forth with brilliant terseness—the way in which in civil association human animals become moral men. Public discussion, the common pursuit of truth on matters of common concern, is indeed to be protected as the absolute that Mill proclaimed it to be. It is not to be protected as mere soliloquy. It is not to be protected as private. It is not to be protected as inalienable right. It *is* to be protected as indispensable to self-government.

THE ABSOLUTE FREEDOM OF PUBLIC SPEECH

The interpretation of any Constitutional provision or any moral principle as an absolute faces rough weather in our own public discussion. Experiences of German and Russian tyrannies, as well as of the conservative rigidity in our own Supreme Court, have left Americans, especially the liberals,[10] alert to spring into action against any claim that an absolute is at hand. So Mr. Chief Justice Vinson, in his *Dennis* opinion, solemnly observed that nothing is more certain in social matters today than that there are no absolutes.[11] It has become almost a ritual for even the libertarian members of the Court to disclaim adherence to an "absolutist" view. To say, "I believe that the First Amendment affords an absolute protection" is taken to mean, "I have decided not to be reasonable about this matter."

And yet John Stuart Mill said, as he concluded his delineation of the proper sphere of liberty, "No society is completely free in which these liberties are not absolute."[12] Mr. Justice Vinson, in the same *Dennis* opinion, spoke of the national security as the "ultimate" value of society in a tone suggesting absoluteness. Mr. Justice Frankfurter, when he has been able —as in the *Sweezy* opinion[13]—to overcome his devotion to judicial self-restraint, has shown clearly his uncompromising devotion to the thoughtful society. Mr. Justice Douglas, in *Zorach v. Clauson*,[14] though supporting a released time arrangement which Mr. Justice Black opposed, declared, "The First Amendment within the scope of its coverage is absolute." Mr. Justice Clark, speaking, as *The New York Times* reported, "as a Presbyterian layman," commented, "No to me means 'No' " in interpreting the First Amendment provision that Congress shall make no law respecting an establishment of religion or prohibiting the free exercise thereof.[15] And formal judicial espousal of the "absolutist position,"[16] as it involves *public* speech, was affirmed by Mr. Justice Black in his James Madison lecture in 1961.[17] Finally, in the suit of Alabama officials against *The New York Times* for an advertisement containing criticism of public officials' conduct during a racial disturbance, the Supreme Court ruled that such criticism could not be curbed unless shown to be malicious.[18] Within and outside judicial circles there has developed a disposition to interpret the First Amendment as meaning "what it says."[19] From this we may take heart as we try to show that philosophic discussion, if not philosophers themselves, should be sovereign in our city.

THE ABSOLUTIST ARGUMENT FROM EXAMPLES

To a generation which has declared itself against absolutes —absolutely—it may be in some measure persuasive to begin with cases. There are many examples of discussion on which there appears to be general agreement that no limitation is in order. In general, speech about politics or about the fulfilment of official duties must be free—speech, for example, that presents a candidate or platform for public consideration. We say this without reservation, even when the speech is uttered by persons of extreme or angry or unpopular views.

We have not thought it proper to inhibit Fascist or Communist speech or political agitation as such; Mr. Chief Justice Vinson was explicit on this in his *Dennis* opinion. When we do argue for restrictions, we do so on the ground that more than speech is involved, that there is in fact criminal action or incitement to action or the employment of words with the effect of force, as in the false cry of "Fire" in the crowded theater.[20]

The examples of speech to which we accord unqualified protection and to which we are committed to giving a full hearing go beyond campaign oratory and recommendations for legislation. They may be retrospective as well as prospective. They are analytic and often recriminatory. They reach to the full social context of political behavior. They concern the conduct of schools and school teachers and school boards. They hold up to public view the behaviors of companies, unions, consumers. They comment on the tendency of any private association, large or small, to affect the public interest. They offer reflections on the kind of society we wish to live in, the influence on our conduct of our morality and our laws. They may well involve the interrelations between morality and art or between these and religion.

Our courts have been moving, with some hesitation, to include various forms of art—plays, movies, books—within the sphere protected by the First Amendment. We understand that some "art," such as that of the French postcard, is not within this sphere. But serious reflections on human life and the role of society and individuals in it have been protected from the censor. The aspects of *Lady Chatterley's Lover* most disturbing to the "moralists" are the ones that seem to bring it into the realm of protected discussion. We are committed, it seems, to the freedom of the forming of our culture, even if we hesitantly tend to label some items as "for adults only." We are moving toward Plato's stress on culture's importance to politics even if we defy Plato in our insistence on the liberty culture should enjoy.

Again, we accord absolute freedom to religion. Whether we do this because we take religion as an activity in itself, distinct from other activity, or because religion is a special case of thinking and speaking, we need not settle here; the Justices of the Supreme Court do not seem of one mind on the matter. In either view we are committed to the free exercise of religion without qualification, whether as we profess faith or criticize such professions. This does not mean that persons can obtrude their religious ceremonies into any place at any time. It does not mean that in the name of religion men can practice what the sense of the community declares separable from religion— polygamy, snake charming, or fraudulent faith healing. But it does mean, to refer once again to Mr. Justice Douglas' dictum in the *Zorach* case, that within its proper range religious expression may not be subjected to even "a little restraint." And what, it is asked, if religion should threaten our internal security, our national defense, our public morale? Our answer is, we do not believe that the free exercise of religion can threaten these. Once it was thought that Catholicism involved international conspiracies in Rome, the "old Moscow." But we have learned to distinguish matters of faith from those of political action. We agree that if a law did abridge the free exercise of religion it would be unconstitutional. We are fortified in our agreement by the specter of totalitarian oppressions of religion.

Though all Constitutional phrases inevitably are terse summaries of grand and complex ideas, one might wish that the First Amendment provision respecting speech had been, like that for religion, expressed in terms of a "free exercise." This might help to distinguish between speech as simple utterance, which certainly must sometimes be restricted, and the "exercise of speech" for which an uncompromising freedom can reasonably be claimed. The exercise of speech, when free, confers upon individual and society the distinctive moral quality to which our Constitution commits us. Public speech, the kind of speech that develops and forms and reforms the public intentions which direct our government—such is the speech which is, when we exercise it, truly an exercise in freedom. This is the exercise of speech which must be free.

To speak of freedom of speech as absolute is to say, "Speech is not to be abridged or restricted; the speaker is not to suffer

or be called to account for its exercise." The public always
wants to hear what its members have to say *on public matters,*
so far as a public decision is thereby informed. But such an
absolute is, of course, embodied in particulars of time and
place. One may not, in the name of the free exercise of speech,
or religion, march into a church service and shout against
churches and preachers, any more than one can stir a panic
in a crowded theater. The ground for restriction may be the
nonpublic character of the utterance; again it may be the irra-
tional, though public, attitudes which are instigated. A rough
principle regarding the particularisations that may be involved
is that except for a quite limited set of well-defined emergencies, men should be unfettered in saying or writing their
thoughts on public affairs where and when and as they think
best. Indeed public speech needs encouragement: there are
not so many places and times available to the ordinary speaker,
and the assurance of an interested audience is not always easy.
For even if listeners must be free not to listen, the public
freedom of speech requires that all speakers have a chance
to reach them. A popular government, and especially its
courts, must see to it that adequate provision is made for all
views to be heard, for all speakers to have their fair chance.
A crucial negative principle thus is the prevention of unequal
treatment of competing theories of public policy. One can
imagine the reaction to a genuine discrimination by the TV
networks against any sizable political group.

The quality of the speech whose exercise must be protected,
absolutely, is defined by its relation to the formation—literally,
the constituting—and the self-government of the public. The
second element in this relation is the more familiar, whether
governors are considered just "servants" of the people, as
Walter Lippmann suggests they now tend to be,[21] or whether
they more independently carry out the popular will at its
sober and rational best—a role which Lippmann assigns to
the strong executive. But the first element in the relation is
the more fundamental: freedom is what is found in that expression which works to constitute a public or, in Paine's
terms, a society. Political speech does this in the first instance,

and as a matter of course, since politics is the community in action. But a community can be active, too, in ways that are less overt. Its activity, insofar as speech is involved in it, includes the preliminaries to actions and also action's ends. Constituting of a community includes thoughts formed and forming, loyalties developing, tastes maturing, interests deepening. It is men becoming thoughtful and responsible citizens. The constituting of the religious communities is one example of such communication; others center about the academy, the theater, the exploration of nature, the arts, athletics. Insofar as men are, in their communications, developing such public aspects of their lives, they are building the foundation of significant moral activity. Speech is not to be protected as "good" on some particular interpretation of "good." It must be protected, rather, because it constitutes a community a moral agent capable of good and bad. It makes a public able to be free in the exercise of its mind and will.

The Constitution as an Absolute

The argument on "absolutes" may be further clarified if we shift attention from the First Amendment to the Constitution as a whole. If one asks an American whether he should give the Constitution his absolute support, one may expect an affirmative if somewhat solemn answer.[22] If we ask a judge whether he follows the Constitution, absolutely, it would indeed be surprising if he did not say yes; still more amazing if he declined on principle to answer. But the questioner may persist, "Will you follow the Constitution if it is wrong?" And to this the judge presumably will say, "Possibly the Constitution is imperfect, but my oath commits me to adhere to it as it is now and, if it is changed, to adhere to it as changed." Adherence to the Constitution as an absolute is in this sense simply doing what one has pledged himself to do. The special businesss of the judge is the fulfilment of the pledge to interpret and apply the Constitution as well as he can.

With this last phrase, however, we may suppose that a second wave of challenge approaches. The modern Sophist, desisting from the stress on change, shifts to the assault from vagueness. "You say you adhere absolutely to the Constitution," he says, "but whose version of the Constitution is it? The Constitution taken in a sense that is unequivocal is so empty as to lose all significance. You can achieve absoluteness, or definiteness, only by retreating from the actual human scene."

It would be ironic indeed if that body of principles which we take to constitute our body politic turns out to be so vague or general as to constitute nothing. That there is real difficulty in a Constitution that is too specific we may readily concede, for in the degree to which it is specific it will take sides for some people against others. The effective rejoinder to the charge that in avoiding this it thins itself to nullity is to be found in identifying the Constitution, or some elements in it, as precisely what makes sense of differing interpretations and opposing views. The question, "Whose view of the Constitution do you defend absolutely?" must in one sense be answered, "My own," with due humor and modesty. But more fundamentally it must be answered, "That which makes this question, and the wide variety of answers to it, intelligible and proper in our common affairs."

The fact that the meaning of the Constitution may always be debated does not mean that it may sometimes be deserted. It does not mean that as one follows it he is simply committed to "his own view." An absolute devotion to the Constitution means an effort to do whatever is needed to get it straight, to discover a meaning that can be publicly justified. This is the basis of the "preferred position" of the First Amendment. The morality of public discussion is the true, the absolute morality in that it is the code that insists upon the consideration of change and persistence, of agreement and difference in Constitutional arrangements. It is this literally constitutive role of such discussion that gives it a special and absolute position in the Constitution. Though all need not, as some would choose to, engage in endless discussions of political theory, still such discussion must be carried on as the framework for all of our more private activities.

To the pluralist contention that there must be variety and

stubborn recalcitrance of individual views, we answer, "Yes, but not to the point of total irrelevance or mutual unintelligibility." Plurality in tastes, habits, ways of making a living —all that individuality which delighted Mill—makes for a lively and interesting community. But there must be community to begin with, and this requires a framework of common understanding.

I am aware of the extent to which I repeat here the Socratic argument against the Sophists. My "apology" for this is that the Sophists seem so recurrently successful in administering the hemlock cup of relativity to the Socrates that is in each of us. The present case against the Sophist must take the form of showing that one can say both, "I am for the Constitution, absolutely," and "I am not sure that I can ever catch the meaning of the Constitution perfectly." Or, with specific reference to public discussion, one must show that he can say, "I am for the freedom that public speech conveys, absolutely," and also "I do not see exactly in every detail what this means." To Socrates it seemed obvious that one can be committed to a goal, ultimately the highest Good, with unreserved determination, and still be prepared to concede personal fallibility in saying what the goal was. One can be, on the moral side, dedicated absolutely to the pursuit and still tolerant of ways to it other than those which one follows himself. One need not regard as damned those whose ways to salvation are different from his own. On the intellectual side, one can subject his own conclusions to the challenge of competing and contradictory alternatives. But this does not of itself invalidate either one's ultimate loyalty or one's need to serve that loyalty, with due tolerance, in his own special way. It is a strange patriot who will not do his best for his country because he is not always sure just what is best for it. The native hue of his resolution demands, rather than is obscured by, the thought that makes his nation's welfare clear.

General Propositions and Particular Cases

The absolutist view also is challenged on the ground that the actual behavior of those who profess it belies their

theoretic profession. This charge is voiced by Mr. Justice
Frankfurter in a note to his concurring statement in *Dennis*.
The absolutists in fact, it is held, after proclaiming an unqualified freedom of public discussion, go on to admit exceptions. They concede, for example, that there are "fighting
words,"[23] libelous words, incitements to violence, that must
be restricted. They are thus caught in the contradiction of
trying to be both absolutist and reasonable. Their embarrassment confirms the tendency of all extreme views to generate
their opposites.

This objection is especially characteristic of many "anti-
absolutists" who are themselves especially devoted to the
freedom of expression. The objection falls, I think, because it
fails to distinguish a general principle from its application in
a particular situation. This failure may be traced, perhaps
illogically, to the famous dictum of Mr. Justice Holmes in
Lochner[24] that general propositions by themselves do not completely determine particular cases. The assertion is often taken
to mean that there must be other nongeneral and tacit
premises which affect the decision. But what Holmes said,
literally, was, "General propositions do not *decide* concrete
cases." A general proposition must always receive concretion.
The office of the generality is not to determine the issue in
shining isolation; it is rather to provide a frame, a definite
limit, which will, as Holmes said, "carry us far toward the
end." The freedom of discussion can be absolute without a
commitment to the unimpeded liberty of all utterance. The
concrete problem is to find a test for our exclusions in terms
of a firm interpretation of the freedom which public speech
confers.

Libertarians have been perplexed about the propriety of
protecting speeches and meetings by American proto-Nazis
like those led by George Lincoln Rockwell. In one case,
there was uncertainty whether the First Amendment should
be construed to protect the dissemination on the streets of
the nation's capital of leaflets which announced the
doom of the city at the hands of Negroes directed by a
Jewish plot. Should such "public discussion" be protected?

Clearly its subject matter and its purpose are of public concern. The leaflets are addressed to the public. They have the form, like the Beauharnais lithographs in Chicago,[25] of a petition for redress of grievances. They constitute argument rather than force aimed at a desired change. On such grounds these expressions must, I am sure, be protected under the First Amendment. Needless to say, the same freedom must be accorded to leaflets circulated by groups of the opposite persuasion.

If now, to continue the story, we conceive the two groups physically approaching one another, at what point do we withdraw the First Amendment protection and prescribe interference? As the groups face each other before the carnage, or as they actually start to conflict, when may—when should —the police step in? We cannot ask that the police wait until heads—probably including some of their own—actually have been broken. We must rely upon the police—and upon the training we should have assured them—to determine when rational exchange in speech in fact has given way to the raw clash of weapons. It is the lot of the police to have to decide "when to break it up"; and the police can make mistakes. But the police must, in our society—and subject always to judicial review—decide when speech no longer is being countered with speech, when the evils to be overcome may not be reduced by further exchange of words, when words are actually being used with the effect of force and must be met by force. It is this kind of situation, as Mr. Justice Jackson observed in his *Dennis* concurring opinion, in which the test of clear and present danger seems capable of reasonably precise application.

Do we then, if we agree that the police may order Rockwell to disband a meeting verging on violence, thereby desert the proposition that the First Amendment absolutely protects the freedom of the exercise of public speech? Certainly not. It may be that some friends of civil liberties will believe that the meeting was too soon terminated and will say therefore that our devotion to free discussion is tepid and sorry. There always is danger that "verging on violence" will be interpreted by the forces of the law to stifle legitimate dissent. But this concerns the application, not the principle. One does not qualify a principle by showing that its application involves judgment—such as the judgment whether in a given situation effective public discussion is possible. Two partisan groups, grimly shooting it out, have no claim on the "freedom of association." Absolute freedom of public speech is distinct from the making of judgments about when such speech ends and force begins.

THE DOCTRINE THAT ONLY "GOOD" SPEECH SHOULD BE FREE

Reference to concerted human waywardness brings to mind once more the theory of the limits of speech which appears in the Call to Public Virtue. That theory is advanced, with sagacity and energy, by Professor Walter Berns, in *Freedom, Virtue and the First Amendment*. As noted above, Berns reviews recent Supreme Court decisions on censorship, riots, Communists, and related topics and finds the Court deficient in not according priority to "virtue" as the end of government. Berns explicitly dissociates himself from intolerance and crude censorship. But his view is no less "moralistic" in its application of criteria for restrictions on speech. "Detective magazines" are to be censored because they are vicious and pornographic. Terminiello should have been silenced because he was a despicable character. American Communists are disloyal and hence have no claim on the rights of free expression, or, alternatively, the social value of their speech is very low. "Bad" speakers, "bad" speeches, do not deserve protection. A government that is properly engaged in raising the moral quality of the community must judge and limit public discussion according to the moral quality of speaker or speech.

Government should indeed play a part in heightening the community's moral quality; government is, after all, a part of the way in which men exercise their reasoning capacities. But the critical element is the meaning assigned to "moral quality." For Berns, as for the others in the Strauss school, there is a set of moral principles which, though hard to state precisely, are yet obligatory upon all reasonable men. "Good" citizens, who can properly claim a citizen's privileges, must be decent, loyal, peaceful. The fallacies in such an appeal to a "rational common-sense morality" already have been exposed. Furthermore, the Berns analysis misses the essential point of government as *self*-government. Speech, so long as it contributes to the forming of the public mind, should be free, for this is indispensable to the direction of the public action by the public intentions. To impose upon everyone a particular standard of decency or loyalty or even good order is to deny self-government. On the other hand, to have the public policy issue from the public deliberation is both self-government and, in the most fundamental sense, virtue as well.

The position taken here is, in historical terms, committed to the Kantian political ethic and so exposed to the objections traditionally brought against that ethic. But in fact few thinkers reject the Kantian formal principles as essential to a conception of virtue. The classic arguments are over their sufficiency. That men should be consistent, and that they should accord to others the dignity they prescribe to themselves, are principles which are generally accepted even if some find them inadequate to provide full ethical instruction. But it seems clear that the attempt to extend a public morality beyond the formal principles is precisely what brings on an imposition of some persons' private standards upon others.

For many thoughtful friends of civil liberty the most difficult question is that associated with disloyalty. Berns, as I have noted, found decisive in the *Dennis* case the low rating to be accorded to Dennis' speech because he was a member of the Communist Party. And Walter Lippmann, in *The Public Philosophy*, holds that "the right to those institutions" of free expression "is . . . for those who adhere to them." Thus, Lippmann continues, "the criterion of loyalty is an indubitable commitment to defend and preserve the order of political and civil rights."[26] The disloyal, Berns and Lippmann argue, have cut themselves out of the basic agreement that supports the process of public discussion. Since they are out of the fundamental agreement they cannot fairly claim to enjoy self-government.

There are real difficulties in Lippmann's insistence upon assurance of due process when that is taken together with his denial of the privilege of free public discussion. Lippmann would assure a public hearing to anyone charged with membership in a "disloyal" organization. But congressional investigating committees have found to their embarrassment that bringing alleged Communists before them often provides publicity for Communist doctrine and a sympathetic presentation of individuals being pushed around by superior force. Investigations of business or of the radical right have encountered similar problems. It is true that the committees have resources on their side for counterpublicity. But this is somewhat beside the main issue. That issue is how one demonstrates loyalty. It is my conviction that any participation in public speech demonstrates loyalty in the fundamental sense. For such a speaker offers ideas concerning the American public and other publics for public deliberation. If he says that we are in a bad way, or that Russia or China is in a good way, we need to consider his evidence. He may not believe what he says, as is the case with many a noncontroversial speaker who merely seeks popularity or votes. But the notable feature of the Communist in America today is the certainty of his unpopularity. This may not guarantee his sincerity but it removes one reason for doubting it.

Still, "there can be no right to destroy the liberal democratic state," says Lippmann,[27] and Berns affirms the familiar anxiety that we may permit disloyal speech to generate an American Lenin or Hitler. With Lippmann's assertion, taken literally, there can be no quarrel. But the crucial question is what "destroying the liberal democratic state" means. In fact, to exclude from public discussion the rather musty Marxist doctrines, or their Stalinist or Leninist versions, is a piece of such "destroying." That from such discussion there may develop a Lenin is highly questionable. Leninism, as it developed in Russia, hardly can be attributed to a prior excess of free discussion. One can argue that had Lenin been effectively jailed or shot in the summer of 1917, he could not have headed the October Revolution. But his success reflected circumstances of which his speaking could hardly be called the crucial component. The development of angry minorities, or majorities, is the result not of free discussion but of injustice or poverty. Those who wish to cure disloyalty need to remove its causes instead of simply applying repressive force to those who point them out. Sensitivity to inequity may be imprudent or misplaced, but it is not per se disloyal.

To say that participation in public discussion is an expression of loyalty is not to say that it is all of loyalty. Every man's ultimate loyalty is properly only to the good and right, and to his country only as the vehicle of his particular pursuit of the right or good life. Each person needs to be encouraged in such loyalty by the presence of other, and inspiring, participants in the pursuit. But to try to influence other men's minds, except as they expose themselves in public speech to the discipline of counterspeech, is truly to invade their freedom as thinking men. This is why, as Mr. Justice Frankfurter said in the flag salute cases, government action is not to be directed at a man's inner life.[28] It is not that purposes may not issue in action. But we distinguish the action we may restrict from the inner state which we may not restrict. If, indeed, our educational process has effectively introduced the exercise of free decision, he whose actions are restrained will comprehend the compatibility of the restraint with his freedom of thought.

Freedom of Speech for American Communists

The distinction between thoughts and actions is crucial in the current debates over the First Amendment's relation to the investigations and prosecutions of alleged subversive activities, especially those of the Communist Party of the United States.[29] To a great extent the disagreements in the Supreme Court have been differences, not about the interpretation of the First Amendment, but about the facts.

The principal cases of the past twenty years have found the two wings of the Court at odds largely over whether the Communist Party is engaged in genuine "political activity." The Court majority, in Douds[30] and Dennis, said it was not.

The minority said it was. Both sides appeared to say that if it were, it should be protected under the First Amendment. Both would denounce the exploitation of majority power such as that employed by the Federalist Party in 1798 to impose reprisals upon a political opposition. In the *Yates* decision,[31] when the review of Communist Party activities was made more explicit than in the earlier cases, the Court came, nearly unanimously, to the conclusion that the facts as presented afforded insufficient grounds for conviction; and the Department of Justice later accepted the same conclusion in dropping the prosecutions remanded by the Supreme Court.

There are indeed important differences in political theory at work, in the Court and in the public. But straightforward interpretation of the First Amendment, as "meaning what it says," has been befogged by the concern that we be not "absolutist." The question whether the Communist Party of the United States, in its actual behavior in the United States, is a dangerous and foreign-dominated conspiracy threatening an immediate reign of violence is a question of fact which requires the closest scrutiny. In answering it we should not be, as Mill would say, "driven from our propriety" into saying, "It is so dangerous, we must fudge on our political freedom."[32] No one would protect, under free speech, plots to blow up City Hall, however much whispered conspiratorial speech they might involve. The specter of such an explosion should not send us scurrying away from our political freedom and into such conclusions as the belief that even criticizing the mayor may encourage people to plot in this way. If a march on City Hall threatens to produce violence it can and must be halted, but the facts must be established in distinction from the unpopularity of the marchers.

There is a particularly impressive discrepancy in the judgment of facts in the landmark *Schenck* case[33] involving the conviction of the secretary of the Socialist Party during World War I. In the opinion which initially formulated the test of clear and present danger, Mr. Justice Holmes announced that Schenck's circulation of antidraft pamphlets to registrants constituted a clear and present danger of substantive evils to the country. But in the *Dennis* case Mr. Chief

Justice Vinson, as he construed the test pursuant to the suggestion of Judge Learned Hand,[34] spoke of the circulation of the pamphlets as an "insubstantial gesture toward insubordination." I am not concerned here to dwell upon the relation between the Vinson and Holmes interpretations of the danger test. What is clear is that they took different views of the facts. And unless one thinks that facts are differently judged only when principles are different, then one must attribute a major part of the Court's disagreements to these differing assessments of what the situation actually is. It is perhaps reasonable to weigh the later judgment of the *Schenck* facts as more objective than the earlier judgment. The urgencies of a "hot war" situation tend to create a bias of perception to which even his admirers do not claim that Mr. Justice Holmes was entirely immune.

The distinction between the judgment of fact and the judgment of policy principle is indeed hard to draw and to maintain. In the work of courts we have our most striking examples of both similarity and difference. A court does not look at random. It has its principles; it looks to see whether the facts fall under them. The very statement of the facts reflects principles, but the facts must for all that involve a stubborn and intractable element external to the principles. It is partly, though not entirely, for this reason that no statement of principle can be regarded as surely stated in terms which are unimpeachable. Another source of fallibility is the convergence of two or more principles which contend for relevance to the judgment. A court always must consider whether its construction of principles and their interrelations makes sense of a changing world. But adjustment must itself follow principles, and the fundamental task, especially for the Supreme Court, is to apply to changing social circumstances that Constitution which provides our standard of judgment, and our ground of interest and relevance, in our public activity.

THE SUPREME COURT AND FREE SPEECH AS CONSTITUTIVE

I may summarize my position by reference to some crucial statements from the so-called "libertarian" wing of the Supreme Court. These judges have espoused what has been called the theory of the "preferred position" of the First Amendment. One of the earliest statements of this view was that of Mr. Justice Cardozo in *Palko v. Connecticut*,[35] where freedom of speech was described as "the matrix, the indispensable condition, of nearly every other form of freedom." In the following year, Mr. Justice Stone, in *United States v. Carolene Products*,[36] identified as especially protected such political processes as "can ordinarily be expected to bring about repeal of undesirable legislation" or are "ordinarily to be relied upon to protect minorities." The presumption in such cases is that free discussion of public matters, as indispensable to the democratic political process, must be "preferred" to other Constitutional values in the event of a conflict.

The "preferred position" as so stated is not an absolutist position, though in practice certain judges have so consistently preferred the First Amendment as to make the position practically absolute. As I have noted earlier, professions of "absolutism" come very uneasily in our political generation, even from Mr. Justice Brandeis, who wrote in his concurring opinion in *Whitney*[37] what is surely our greatest single judicial statement on freedom of speech. Happily Mr. Justice Black has now declared in his James Madison lecture that he affirms the absolutist stand, to say that the First Amendment is intended "to withdraw from the Government all power to act" in the area of public speech.[38] I would not wish to ascribe to Mr. Justice Black the details of the argument developed here. But his example encourages me to think that the courts and the public will make articulate the identification of public discussion with American self-government.

No doubt the term "absolutist" conveys a wide variety of meanings. Some of these meanings are surely such as thoughtful men will condemn. Some, despite critical doubts, I believe we should frankly avow. I suppose that my argument is roughly summed up in the familiar thesis that we should not become antidemocratic in trying to protect ourselves from the antidemocrats. The assertion is sound, even if unrefined. It says, in effect, that having found the best that we can be, we can try for nothing else. It affirms a necessary connection between survival and integrity. So when the critic says, "This freedom may be the end of us," we answer, like Socrates, that if to remain our best selves we must die, then die we will; but in fact we believe that fidelity to our best principles makes us most likely to live.

To speak of an absolute in conduct is not to consecrate rigidity. It is rather to speak of a principle which is constant as its particular embodiment shifts. Those only have difficulty in comprehending this who see only change, who do not understand that all reasoned activity is this combination of the passing and the persistent. "To thine own self be true" is not invalidated by the fact that men grow or by the transiency of many interests. Absolutes are compatible with change. They make change intelligible. Truly, only the permanent changes.

THE CONSTITUTION AND AMERICAN INDIVIDUALISM

There still is a last and in some ways most imposing wave of objection to meet, different from the challenges of the Sophists and the men of Public Virtue. Another absolute appears to offer opposition, and this is the sober conscience of Thoreau. Can you, he asks, be true to the Constitution when it is unjust? When it supports immoral taxes or compels the return of the fugitive slave? Can anyone, seriously, affirm absolute allegiance to any public being, to anything other than the dictates of his own individual conscience? Are not the entire public, its opinions, its Constitution, contrivances to serve private purposes, an instrument to be adapted as necessary with prudence and flexibility?

Criticizing Thoreau is somewhat like putting freedom of thought in jail, and it is only partly redeemed by recollection of how Thoreau spent his time inside the walls. But in fact the lesson from Concord must yield to the Athenian doctrine enunciated by Socrates that the freedom of inquiry rests on public rather than private considerations. The appeal to individual conscience, when construed to deny obligation to the public, is untenable.

The conscientious objector sometimes phrases his dispute with the public as being an argument between principle and force. Thoreau spoke in that manner, on occasion, but he said wiser things too. He believed that reasoning men can talk together, can appeal rationally to one another, and that a reasoning public can be formed. Like Thoreau and his fellow prisoner, men can exchange thoughts and still next day depart, each to hear his private locust sing. Moral quality need not be limited to wholly private affairs.

From the "public" side it also is sometimes contended that those who object to public policy on grounds of conscience must be cowardly or crazy. There probably are rascals and fools among conscientious objectors, as in most ranks of men, but objectors only carry to an extreme that dispraise of force which nearly all affirm in some degree in human affairs. Merely denouncing the appeal to conscience hardly forwards successful public discussion.

Can one persuade Thoreau and his spiritual descendants of today that the Constitution deserves to be supported with the absoluteness which they assert for the individual conscience? One might, if he could convince them that their own position is intrinsically social. We may not persuade them to be public officials, or even to respect public officials, but we may convince them that the better society they hope for can be had only if their communication has its chance. We need to show them that our kind of public is the condition of access of *Walden* and *On Civil Disobedience* to American minds. We have to convey to them the conception of a public which is both condition of rational sociability and itself also amenable to criticism. Such a public can mediate the relations which constitute our morality; in such activity the public and private concerns come together.

The Thoreau argument appears in recent Supreme Court litigation involving the right of individuals to defy investigation of what they claim to be their private affairs. The defiant individualist, if he puts his case on merely individual grounds, is outnumbered and irrelevant. As an individual he is just one against an indefinite array of others whom the government represents. As an individual speaker, he does not reach the public's argument. He may show courage, or just stubbornness, but this cannot be legally effective. On the other hand, his defiance may find a thoroughly valid defense on public grounds. He may refuse to disclose to a congressional committee how he votes, or what he reads, on the basis that such coerced disclosure corrupts the process of public discussion. Accountability to public officials in matters of public speech and voting is inconsistent with self-government. A man may indeed be held responsible for making known his views at the proper time. He may, if he is a public official, be questioned on all matters relevant to the discharge of his public duties; and these do not, of course, include revelation of thoughts as distinct from actions. The public opinion that should govern a democratic public must be spontaneous. On all matters which are related to participation in the political processes that form the public, individuals must be free to reveal their opinions as they choose and when they choose. Unhappily, in recent cases,[39] the Supreme Court has been unwilling to identify securely those associative processes which we must have if our public is to be self-governing.

Men may, for the public's sake, sometimes refuse to talk when it might well be easier for them, as private individuals, to speak and be let go. They may refuse because they believe that talking under the wrong conditions obstructs the forming of the self-governing society. They may hold that when men talk together rightly they are civil, that when they talk under duress they achieve only incivility and public nuisance. Of course, the man who stands in contempt of a court or committee will go to jail. And we may not censure the authorities for assuming the power to put him there. We may blame them for stupidity, but not for their fidelity to the law. In a public composed of men rather than angels there always will be such irreducible moral conflicts even when there is good will on both sides. The individual may be morally right in not cooperating, as the judge is legally—and morally—right in sentencing him. The most we can say is that patience, humor, and continued discussion will minimize the frequency and severity of such collisions.

To ask that judges accept an absolute is not to suggest that they assume the mantle of infallibility. Let us consider the case of a man who defies an investigating committee because, as he claims, he is being coerced to reveal his religious beliefs. The committee, we may suppose, says to him: "Well, as to your religion, you have a right to be silent. But there is no question of religion here." The committee, we may further suppose, asserts that not religion but fraudulent representation about healing powers is the central issue, as in the *Ballard* case,[40] or that polygamy is involved, as in *Davis v. Beason*.[41] If then the individual still contends that religion is involved, what can the absolutist say? He may reply, first, that the disagreement can be phrased and understood only if there is some common principle—such as "religion is not to be inquired about"—which absolutely governs the case; and second, that it is in the nature of the human situation that this absolute will be interpreted differently by different persons. In such a situation the stronger party, or that with the more inclusive political authority, will in fact or in law prevail. And the other party will feel put upon, unjustly treated. But such a complaint as he may reasonably submit must be made in terms of such a common principle as we have asserted. He is justified in complaining if any human being, citizen or official, asserts infallibility and refuses argument. But the very recognition of fallibility implies an absolute against which human knowledge is measured. Our political institutions are set up, fundamentally, to commit us to the endless pursuit of what we may approach but never surely attain.

The Wisdom of Learned Hand

It is fitting to conclude this effort to show how free public speech may bring public and private affairs into congenial continuity by paying tribute to one more hero in the never-ending struggle for political freedom. This hero is Judge Learned Hand, self-styled pragmatist, who, despite his worldly wisdom, or because of it, wrote in the spirit of a sane and fundamental idealism. As Judge Hand, from his position outside the Supreme Court, profoundly influenced that Court and the general course of our constitutional law, so in his mellow and philosophic writings he set down the democratic premises upon which our freedom depends.

As Learned Hand told his story in *The Spirit of Liberty,* he was instructed at Harvard in the errors of neo-Hegelian idealism. William James and Oliver Wendell Holmes, Jr., taught him to be a pragmatic pluralist, devoted to the elective system in colleges and outside them too. Whatever the influence of this theoretic background, we find Judge Hand, in Federal District Court in 1917, writing our most impressive wartime interpretation of the First Amendment.[42] In that opinion he defined and prescribed, without qualification, the distinction between "agitation, permissible as such," and "incitement." He moved somewhat away from the strictness of this early view, as we find him in the 1940's formulating what has been called the "grave and probable danger" version of the Holmes danger test.[43] And in his more theoretical writings on politics he expressed with his customary urbanity and humor serious doubts about the reality of such a thing as a common will.

Judge Hand clearly can speak the language and command the attention of the pluralists. But this makes particularly significant the following paragraph on democracy's premises:

And so when I hear so much impatient and irritable complaint, so much readiness to replace what we have by guardians for us all, these supermen, evoked from somewhere in the clouds, whom none have seen and none are ready to name, I lapse into a dream, as it were. I see children playing on the grass, their voices are shrill and discordant as children's are, they are restive and quarrelsome; they cannot agree to any common plan; their play annoys them; it goes so poorly. And one says, let us make Jack the master, Jack knows all about it; Jack will tell us what each is to do, and we shall all agree. But Jack is like all the rest; Helen is discontented with her part and Henry with his, and soon they fall again into their old state. No, the children must learn to play by themselves; there is no Jack the master. And in the end, slowly and with infinite disappointment they do learn a little; they learn to forbear, to reckon with another, accept a little where they wanted much, to live and let live, to yield where they must yield; perhaps, we may hope, not to take all they can. But the condition is that they shall be willing at least to listen to one another, to get the habit of pooling their wishes. Somehow or other they must do this if the play is to go on.[44]

In this "must," this categorical imperative of listening, of "pooling wishes," Learned Hand identifies our absolute morality of public discussion. Within itself, the law of that discussion is the readiness of speaker and listener to attend without reservation to one another, and for the community as a whole it is precisely this process which confers moral quality upon the social body. Freedom is the excellence which can bless the continuing play when these rules are known and observed.

V

American Freedom and the Wider World

THE AMERICAN PUBLIC knows itself, superficially, more readily in foreign relations than in domestic affairs. In some sense, as we move among the nations, we are one agent, one public aware of its component elements, its powers, its responsibilities. In fact our behaviors show little serious evidence of such awareness. Though we have in this century moved uneasily into the role of leading world power, we have been slow to formulate a public morality to govern our relations with other countries. Freedom has seemed to reside simply in absence of relation, rather than in informed interaction. The initial separating and isolating impulse has continued to dominate our moral theories of politics even though the isolation is physically no longer real.

In our thinking about international affairs, as in our domestic attitudes, we have developed a folklore which is dear to us but which serves us poorly. That folklore is deeply isolationist. With no particular arrogance, we have regarded as especially our own our democracy, our self-government, our freshness and honesty. We may be innocents abroad, but ours is the innocence of complete virtue rather than of inexperience. Had the elder nations halted? We took up the lesson and the burden, in our confident pioneering youth, in our freedom from the weary shrewdness of European intrigue. There are, in this folklore, three kinds of countries in the world: the old, too far gone in self-interest to be saved; the young, hardly mature enough to know political right from wrong; and the United States of America. On such a conception, how could we do better than keep free of foreign entanglements?

131

However crude this stereotype, its influence has been profound. Now, circumstances of equal crudity conspire to dispel it. We need to replace it with realistic but also morally intelligible conceptions of our place in the wider world: as before, I shall try to locate such a theory as a middle path between the "moral right" and the "moral left."

If freedom is not conceived as simply the absence of restraint, if freedom is found in fidelity to right principles—principles of our own natures rather than handed down to us from on high—then America can be free abroad only as she achieves with others the same qualities of self-government which are imperative at home. It is not America alone who is to be free, it is the wider undertakings which cross national boundaries and respond to interests and purposes of a common international character. Here as before the discovery of a public which can be free is the discovery of a common morality to which the parties can adhere in fulfilment of their own deepest aspirations.

The Retreat from Moralism

Present dilemmas in our moral thinking about foreign policy were defined in the period of World War I, in the controversy that still rages about the mind and career of Woodrow Wilson. American presidents since 1920 have been at pains to frame their foreign policies in terms of avoiding Wilson's alleged mistakes. On the one hand, they must avoid the "excess moralism" which led Wilson to follow his own Presbyterian ethic with dogmatic disregard of political realities. On the other hand, they must not, innocently, permit the free play of such bitter and vengeful motives as those of the British and French delegates at Versailles. Above all they must not fall into what some regard as Wilson's consummate hypocrisy of proclaiming obligations which he knew to be "impractical." The lesson of these criticisms has been thought to be a moral neutralism which confines our public morality to our own affairs.

The detailed analysis of Wilson's successes and failures is beyond the scope of this discussion, but I must declare my own belief that Wilson survives such arguments much better than do his critics. The essential information on our efforts to stay out of the war, on our entry into it, on our relations with revolutionary Russia, and on Wilson's policies at Paris provide convincing evidence that though he made mistakes they were at the level of immediate judgments on particular facts.[1] Wilson led American public opinion with clarity and firmness both about entering the war and about fighting it, and he was dramatically near success in 1919 in his effort to overcome the long-standing isolationist tendencies of the United States. Doubtless he might have been more conciliatory in 1919, but our failure to join the League is to be blamed on his embittered opponents rather than on his failure to assuage their bitterness.

In the continuum of political theories Wilson belongs in the valid center position; in foreign policy matters in 1914 we may attribute the extremes to the stands taken by Theodore Roosevelt and Robert M. LaFollette. Roosevelt was the crusader, hot on the trail of human evil abroad with the zest that marked his lion hunting in Africa, his trust hunting at home. LaFollette, equally moral in his middle western isolationism, was deeply sceptical about extending to our foreign relations the morality that inspired his brilliant reform career in Wisconsin. I do not mean to press these analogies too far. But certainly, as between these two, Wilson approached our foreign relations as a moral problem without compromising the heart of his Presbyterian creed—the recognition of men's capacity for self-government.

Wilson often is regarded as committed to a metaphysical insistence on a rigid moral code derived from self-evident truths. But Wilson was trained in British and Hegelian historicism. When he went to Paris he took with him the ablest staff he could assemble to study crucial areas of Europe and Asia with a view to deciding what the self-determining units of a new political order could and should be. He made policy mistakes, as he conceded, like the premature cession of the Tyrolese territory to Italy, but this is hardly surprising in the light of all the Conference's complexities. The Monday morn-

ing quarterbacks have had many a Monday to point out how
the job might have been done better. But as they do so they
do not, as a rule, reject Wilson's principles; rather, they invoke
those criticisms as they lament their "betrayal."

American presidents should indeed be "realistic," should
consider the views of senators, members of the opposing
political party, foreign counterparts, and so on. They should
of course display a proper respect for the other participants
in the governing process. Wilson did these things, perhaps not
exactly as we would do them now. And he maintained a moral
grandeur of view which we need sorely to recover. Our disappointment over the League's failure and our international
anxieties since 1920 are fully intelligible only as we understand that we measure our own success by the principles
which Wilson followed.

There is one phase of Wilson's foreign policy which illus-
trates this with particular clarity, and this is his attitude toward
Russia between 1917 and 1919. His sympathy with the initial
efforts against autocracy was outspoken and need not be
attributed simply to a prudent interest in keeping Russia in
the war. He saw without illusion how important it was to
maintain Russia's freedom from intervention as she tried to
settle her own internal disorders. He resisted stubbornly the
plans of the Allies for extensive military intervention; he did
his best to give the new regime its chance to be broadly based
and democratically effective. He did not regard Marxist and
Leninist principles as the work of the devil; only after re-
peated efforts had failed to halt the descent into dictatorship
and terror did he come to despair of diplomatic dealings with
the Soviet government. The tragedy of our times is that a like
level-headedness did not so far pervade the policy of the other
Allies that Russia and her revolution might have been saved
for the West.

I touch on this history in order to illustrate a "middle road"
position in respect to the morality of our foreign relations. The
most impressive criticism of recent policy toward Russia has
come from George F. Kennan, who has assailed the "mor-
alistic-legalistic" cast in which—as he believes—much of that

policy has been phrased.[2] Kennan deplores preaching; he urges that we confine our moral proposals to what we really can manage. He has led the way in assailing "undue moralism."[3] But in his own positive recommendations for policy, Kennan offers a thesis thoroughly in keeping with the austere principles of Wilsonian self-determination.[4] He tells us that the only serious political instruction we can offer Russia is our example; we are not going to compel or talk Russia into a Public Virtue exactly like ours. He predicts that as a new political order is stabilized in Russia it will not be very similar to ours, especially in respect of its attention to "individualism." Yet Kennan affirms his hope for such desirable steps in Russian development as the relaxation of present regulations governing foreign travel inside Russia and travel of Russians abroad, of curbs on political criticism, and of the evangelistic export of communism. Given such developments, Kennan believes, the greatness and profound humanity of the Russian people might become effective in Russia's relations with other peoples. The Russian cause is not ultimately alien to that of other men, even Americans.

NATIONAL INTEREST AND MORAL DIGNITY

We may find escape from our post-Wilson negations if we follow the lead offered by Professor Hans Morgenthau. Writing in the *American Political Science Review*, in December, 1950, Morgenthau asserted that "the choice is not between moral principles and the national interest devoid of moral dignity, but between one set of moral principles, divorced from political reality, and another set of moral principles, derived from political reality."[5] Morgenthau's answer to the choice is clear; the crucial question is how we are to understand the "divorce" and the "derivation."

The position that follows "moral principles divorced from political reality" is the foreign policy counterpart of what I have termed the Call to Public Virtue. This has "roots in reality." But the reality is of a very special type. It is not the reality of the actual men by whom international politics is conducted. The reality to which the Call to Public Virtue appeals is supposed to reside in the true Nature of Man. Actually, it is likely to resemble closely the empirically known social life of small and intimate groups. Morgenthau is arguing, as I understand him, that one can think clearly about the morality of international politics only as he leaves behind him the parochiality of the standards of the local society. Or, on the formal level, he is urging that one must do more than read from Human Nature if he is to come to effective knowledge of better and worse in foreign affairs. The reality to be considered is the day-by-day tangle of practical politics and the men in it.

Certainly Americans have been accustomed to measuring foreigners by American standards. With us, as with others, the expression "foreign devil" is redundant. In the spirit which animates the Call to Public Virtue we have sent forth our missionaries to impart American principles to inhabitants of other lands. Enterprises both heroic and stupid have sought to wean the heathen from wood and stone. Our emissaries, sometimes with patience and tolerance, sometimes with impatience and bigotry, sometimes eager for and sometimes indifferent to self-government among "the natives," have exhibited at large the American moral parochialism that can conceive no gods other than ours.

Nor have our attitudes been really different toward those "mature" countries with whom we have associated in war and peace. The record of the world wars is a score of rising crescendo in moral condemnation of our enemies. It is dramatic and saddening to read the story of American estimates of European nations in the great wars, in which we moved from initial desire to sympathize with "legitimate national ambitions" to the discovery of inherent evil in our enemies and amoral national interest in our friends and ourselves. And the tragedy is deeper in that it is in these war attitudes, with all their brittle and transitory brightness, that our principal mobilizations of moral energy have taken place. We have not a mature moral philosophy to guide our relations with other countries.

This is why many Americans, especially those whose minds

are on business or national security, have followed the second alternative described by Morgenthau and have formulated our foreign policy position in terms of "national interest devoid of moral dignity." This is a natural extension of the radical pluralist conviction that admits as valid only the interests of small voluntary groups. At an extreme this view probably is held by slave traders; in sophisticated form it may be the approach of the "enlightened capitalists" who exploit the "underdeveloped" countries. It is not "immoralist." It disclaims any expectation of finding moral community with foreign peoples; it expects them to try to get the best of us and hopes for no more than a durable exchange of services. Countries, companies, individuals are so many devices for getting the day's work done. It is sufficient to devote one's energies to tangibles like oil and military defense; self-government and respect for persons are for home consumption.

It is this view which is, as Morgenthau puts it, occupied with the national interest, devoid of moral dignity. In rejecting it, Morgenthau advocates the alternative of a set of moral principles "derived from political reality." He invites us, accordingly, to identify securely the political reality that is involved and also the meaning properly to be assigned to "derivation." As I have referred somewhat critically to our missionaries, it may be in order to suggest that in their happiest perceptions of local cultures they offer us effective introduction to the concrete meanings in these crucial terms. In treating the heathen as not wholly blind—though still heathen—they provide the basis for a dignified assertion of moral diversity.

Formally, it is clear that we can "derive" a demand for moral dignity in our foreign policy only as we actually discover morality, including the capacity for moral judgment, in our effective foreign transactions. We tend to phrase this as a discovery of the moral capacity of other people (the creature *is* a man, not a bear!). But it is the interaction that is important, quite apart from questions of moral conceit. The only "derivation" in moral matters that is valid is derivation from morality, or moral potential. I do not speak here of a complete and detailed code of moral judgments. I do refer to that core of moral meaning which includes responsibility, the making and keeping of promises, adherence to general principles in foreign affairs.

In other words, we are speaking here of the capacity to be moral in general, rather than the fulfilment of a particular set of moral standards. From the realities of international exchange there can be derived only a very broad set of moral principles. Just as the existence of many small-group moralities restricts our own public morality to a formal ethic, so the varieties offered on the wider human scene reinforce the logical case for formal ethics at large.

Such a formal association of national interest with dignity is, I believe, in the spirit of reflective realists like Morgenthau and Kennan. Both are suspicious of arbitrary ascriptions of moral obligations, such as may arise from national principles peculiar to one's own country. Both are concerned that we not, in the name of elusive and unbased "international principles," desert that national interest which is after all an indispensable condition of any influence for morality that we can exercise. But both argue from the premise of a basic community among societies—a community resting upon the capacity of men to achieve some moral quality in their common affairs.

Only experience can tell us how far any given collection of men can constitute a community which can govern itself according to general laws. John Stuart Mill reminded us of this early in *On Liberty* and plausibly proposed the criterion of improvability by discussion as a guide to policy. Mill added further, and doubtless with British India in mind, that toward such groups of men as could not govern themselves the only justifiable approach is one which promotes capacity for self-government as swiftly as possible. And such indeed has been the theory of the matter underlying the establishment by the League of Nations and the United Nations of mandated territories and trusteeships.

The foreign policy approach that is both moral and realistic accepts "as real" the existing conduct of international dealings but still "derives" from that conduct the prescription of such policies as convey moral dignity and respect. The reality which provides the major premise includes the capacity for self-criticism and moral judgment. A characteristic policy problem which we face now is that of considering how we may aid or cooperate with another country. There are irreducible elements of difference, doubtless, in manners and morals; and we must accept their ways when these embody enduring value. We cannot insist that they institute a Protestant ethic and free enterprise capitalism. But we can ask that our understandings with them be kept; we can require as a condition of aid and cooperation that such aid as we give contribute to human dignity and comfort. If we conclude that we cannot count on this—and the fault may be in us as well as them—there still is the question of what we do, and in human affairs we are never done with advancing the conditions of morality even when moral exchange itself is not immediately possible.

There are limits to what we can do in economic terms, but in educational assistance, especially in technical and scientific matters, there really are no limits. We will not change folkways much, especially if we try. The task of confirming or initiating moral exchange among nations is an endlessly renewed undertaking in the discovery of what genuinely can be done in common to lift men from the burdens of immediate circumstance. Americans who have become wistful over their displacement as the "newest" country by scores of other nations may well find a wholly new challenge in defining effectively the new forms of relations which they can sustain with other countries. For the seriously moral man or country the good is never achieved—only being achieved.

Moral quality in foreign affairs is a problem, not only in relations with "new nations," but also—and more stubbornly —in relations with those recognized as politically mature. Kant was fond of quoting the European monarch who said, speaking of another ruler, "What my brother wants, I want too." Recognition of morality in another may not foster community; often the very interest of one country in something, land or trade, stimulates in others the impulse to compete. Since 1946, many Americans and many Russian Communists have taken this view of American-Russian relations. The gains of the one have been reckoned losses to the other in the cold war balance sheet.

It is difficult to estimate how much damage to rational human dealings has been caused by the disposition in Russia to fear any evidence of respect for the United States, and by the popularity in our country of berating any view that was not "anti-Communist." The pessimism inherent in this American propensity is expressed in both the impatience of the moralists who Call to Public Virtue and the scepticism of the pluralists who praise only the private association. The former find the available morality in the world all on their side. They cannot see any good in Communists, and that is all there is to say. The pluralists do not try for moral judgment; they look upon Communists dispassionately, as on red ants or avalanches. Both extremes ignore what in fact we have long understood. One has only to read, for example, the dispatches between Washington and our Moscow embassy in 1916 and 1917 to recognize how earnestly we hoped that the genuine morality of the Russian people might dominate the Revolution. We may object with deep conviction to the social program of communism, but that program still is an effort by men to meet a perplexing human problem.

I do not intend to suggest that moral considerations alone are today dominant in our foreign policy. The dreadful pressures of military danger drive us as urgently as do our moral sensitivities to moderate the excesses of both the moralistic and the realistic points of view. It is somewhat pathetic to watch ourselves stumbling between the insistence that of course we are "innocent as doves,"[6] loved by all right-thinking nations, and the recognition that we must be crafty as serpents in lining up all the help we can. External and internal confusions alike work to make us uncertain whether we have, as a nation, any common moral cause to make with other people. We are not clear whether the American public good is "for export." As we think about our evangelism in the First World War, our disillusioned efficiency in the Second, we are perplexed about the terms in which we should formulate our efforts to prevent a third. We do not know how far it is, for us, a moral problem which we must face alone.

CAN AMERICA REMAIN A SOVEREIGN NATION?

The argument has proposed to locate freedom in the active concert which is a self-governing public. Political theories such as this have shared with Rousseau the onus of the charge of extreme nationalism. If the national community is the basis and focus of political obligation, the critics say, then the community cannot itself be subject to wider obligations. It becomes a law unto itself and knows no reason for deference to other societies. It is "sovereign." Rousseau, indeed, complained that his countrymen seemed more European than French.

Doubtless one group's claims upon our moral energies reduce the proportion of those energies available to other groups. But the self-governing nation which accepts the voluntary groups while keeping them responsible is compatible with development of obligations on the wider scene as well. Parochial nationalism is typically the product of a monolithic social morality. It is not congenial with the complex of multiple loyalties which our Constitution legitimates. A country which is bent upon making the most of human capabilities, of bringing out the talent for self-government wherever it may be found, is not the enemy of self-government in other countries, whether they are old or young. Men, alone or in groups, are inevitably the objects most interesting to other men. If America has found it fascinating, as well as strenuous, to undertake within itself the assimilation of many cultures, it can look forward with equal zest to developing fruitful and significant relations abroad. We have indeed our own house to keep in order. But history now has worked to turn our economic and educational enterprises toward the outside world. Only an exclusive and possession-minded nationalism will try to fence itself in. The public morality that enlarges and extends our private values has in principle nowhere on earth to stop.

Some Americans think such an attitude is dangerous and

others think it foolish. Those think it dangerous who have read the "collectivists" out of the human race. Those think it foolish who have become desperate at the political confusions in so many human societies. The premise common to the two is the belief that our self-government is peculiarly our own style and is not for other people. The fallacy which these two views share is their refusal to recognize how similar we are to other countries in respect of both collectivist tendencies and political confusions.

Americans have indeed reason to be proud of our self-government. But we need to distinguish its essence from its accidental aspects and to consider how that essence is to be cultivated. What the particular forms of self-government may be in Russia or China or Cuba or England need not be a matter of moral concern to us. The concretions of human self-direction must be variable. The achievements of self-government will vary also in degree; and international arrangements may properly take account of such variations. Apart from concern for our own survival, our regard for human dignity moves us to promote the participation of men everywhere in governing their own lives. It is neither dangerous nor foolish to work for the principle of self-government, in Russia or Cuba or the Congo, provided that we accord due attention to the same cultural freedoms we practice at home.

Detailed working out of international attitudes toward national freedoms is first of all the proper task of the United Nations. We have led that organization by our military power and the number of votes we could muster. These sources of influence will diminish; in the long run only the force of moral community with other countries can maintain our standing. The undertaking promises to be as interesting as it is urgent. It surely requires neither decking the United Nations in red, white, and blue nor declaring only a commitment to a colorless regulation of secondary interests; it requires, rather, discovery and development of common activities in which our moral energies are genuinely engaged.

To the objection that America's membership in the United Nations qualifies America's sovereignty, we must answer, "Of course." Our foreign policy-making is limited by our membership, even when account is taken of the unanimity provision. But this is only one of many limitations on American "sovereignty." We limit it also when we assure liberties to individuals or groups. In the domestic context, to be sure, it is the public agencies who decide what limits to impose on themselves. In the United Nations, on the other hand, we may be outvoted; our money, our men, perhaps, are at the disposal of an association we do not fully control. We face the question of how far we will find this tolerable as the balance of power shifts in the Assembly. It will be tolerable insofar as it expresses that interest in a public freedom which is the ultimate ground of all our public institutions.

We can and no doubt will maximize our independence of action by military and diplomatic policies. But in the present world situation, that independence will in any case be limited —and more if we withdraw from the United Nations than if we stay in it. In the first instance the restrictions upon us are imposed not by world law but by force. The United Nations is the medium for seeking rationality in relations with other countries: it offers us a chance to compensate for our numerical inferiority. Through the United Nations we can foster the economic and educational activities which can constitute us "world leader" in the way which a respect for self-government requires. As we take the leadership from the hands of the British, we surely can profit from their successes and their failures. It is possible—though desperately difficult —for us to manage to match the diminution of our legal and military supremacy with a corresponding advance in our moral influence. In a world suspicious and resentful of the rich and the strong, we may contrive to become and remain popular. We may be able to provide the initiative in a genuinely popular international government, in a genuine world public.

AMERICA AND THE WORLD'S BUSINESS

Our relations with the rest of the world throw light on how far and in what ways our government should intervene in economic affairs. Business in America never has been shy about asking for protections which, according to theory, are reserved for infants. On the other hand, there always have been resolute theorists who have denounced tariffs and other interferences with competition. Here, once more, the extremes of theory seem implausible. That the government should act to help maintain the "American way of life" or the American standard of living, or that it should have a mind to maintaining Americans in their "ordinary callings," seems too clear to require extended argument. But we would not defend freezing the allocation of American resources in a manner completely unresponsive to the demands of an international division of labor. We need pragmatic working rules rather than rigid programs. We need to seek the kind of mutuality of which a genuine Common Market might offer an example. We need to bear in mind, too, that local arrangements, whatever their scope, tend to raise walls against outsiders even as internal barriers go down. We need to be reasonably conservative in recognizing men's devotion to what they have labored to produce; we need to be able to associate change with adequate provision for relocation and redevelopment of human talents. We need to keep in mind that efficient satisfaction of consumer demand is only one among many significant human aims.

As in the case of the domestic economy, the important requirements are two: assurance of appropriate authority, and circulation of requisite publicity; they are indeed inseparable. The scope of the economic problems must be matched by political machineries. Rich nations will shoulder more of the burden than the poor. The assumption of the burden must be made intelligible by full knowledge of what we are doing. If American labor sees no more than competition with "low-paid foreign workers," it will be loath to support policies encouraging free trade. Advance toward an international economy with an effective division of labor requires that both labor and capital see not only their immediate inconvenience but the larger and more rewarding economy. The sense of the common human undertaking can function as an impressive force provided it is associated with prospects of a common improvement. Americans are interested in the welfare of others—not in the sense of proposing to share with them on literally even terms, but in the sense of hoping to join with them in that human progress which is a necessary condition of a moral political order.

As we consider the bewildering clamor of economic needs across the earth's surface, we will do well to recur for instruction to Adam Smith. In describing the original economy of the American colonies, Smith stressed the relatively high value of labor in the light of the preponderant supply of unworked land. Comparable importance presumably would be assigned by Smith today to those specially trained human "factors" which are the distinguishing possessions of the "developed" countries. The prime aim of our foreign economic policy must be to help in the development of this and other kinds of "capital." To do this may often seem to ignore pressing consumer needs and to cross the intentions of new "democratic" governments. But it seems the only escape from the deadly population-starvation cycle. We cannot impose our own conceptions of policy on other nations, but we can make such a principle an element of any aid which we concert with them.

In the development of capital accumulation abroad, whether in men or machinery, we have impressive resources in our private and semiprivate enterprises. Encouraging economic and educational enterprises abroad and holding them to account in terms of our national purpose constitute a government responsibility as yet little explored. But here the national import of our private undertakings is so obvious that questions of economic or academic freedom seem frivolous. Here again discrepancies between the pursuit of private gain and the promotion of public good are readily identifiable. But, as in the domestic economy, there has been evolving a viable three-cornered competition between public agencies, both national and international, and the activities of private concerns.

OTHER PEOPLE'S SCHOOLS

Assisting the schools of other countries is more important than helping their business. This is not because it is cheaper

to play Socrates than to play Santa Claus. It is rather because
it affords a chance to participate with others in programs
which strengthen the capacity for self-government. The creation of those knowledges, political, economic, and technical,
which will forward the achievement of durable popular rule
must be our principal concern as we work with the "new"
nations. As we do this we need to bear in mind that the education is mutual, not "for them" only.

There is every reason for such educational efforts to be continuous with that federal support which we accord to our
own academic institutions. The same problems will appear
in the form of private influences on the schools. There will
be the same tendencies to limit such assistance to narrowly
scientific and technical forms of instruction. But in principle
we must be prepared to assist the schools of aspiring new nations both with money and also with broadly qualified members of our own teaching profession.

In the efforts of such educators, and notably in the labors
of the Peace Corps, there accrues to our own thinking significant reflection about America's powers and America's limitations. To us who have been the bearers of the standard of
indefinite perfectibility and the holders of practically inex-
haustible resources of human and natural energies, it is fitting
that there be presented the challenge of appreciating and
dealing with the predicament of others less favored. The flash
of the brief, bright climax between Hiroshima and the first
Russian nuclear bomb, when our power seemed to match our
wealth in dominating the world, has faded. Since then we
have come to live with hostile atomic power, and we have
seen the Communist countries achieve the rate of economic
growth which we have not maintained since early in this
century. Recognition of finiteness is not new, but its present
economic and military forms are especially urgent. It points
all the more clearly to the importance of the scientific and
intellectual leadership we may achieve.

There is no very high achievement in being "first" in anything except dignity and understanding. Dignity cannot, however, be resolved in the modern world into unassuming sim-

plicity. It entails rather the mustering and applying of the relevant practical knowledge. Such knowledge our educational enterprise abroad may well stimulate and expand. Presumably it will range from free textbooks and school lunches to interminable conferences between American and local educators about the aims, procedures, materials, and equipment. And we will surely learn as much as we teach, in the revelation of the variety of foreign cultures, the subtlety of personal and political relations which those cultures have worked out in ways very different from our own.

In this process the United Nations ought to play a major role. Participation in such broad and basic programs as elimination of illiteracy has importance in itself as well as strengthening the world organization. UNESCO activities need steady expansion in the form of extensive institutes in which the needs and resources of member countries are reviewed. There would be no prejudice in these to our own special projects involving our own academic persons and programs in direct association with those of other countries.

There are familiar political and moral problems. The former are posed by the countries who lean to the "other side" in the cold war. Congress settles such problems, in the main, by regarding aid or consultation with either Socialist countries or Russia's allies as "giving comfort to the enemy." And in view of our limited resources, it may be imprudent not to spend all we have for "our friends." The heathen without our gates may be thought not our responsibility, even if his salvation offers the greatest challenge. But in fact both self-interest and the demands of human dignity bring us to situations in which we will wish to join an "enemy" in the development of knowledge useful to us both. We may learn by such knowledge; we may exploit the venture to moderate hostility; most of all we may convey to the world a serenity of confidence which we do not promote by huddling tensely on our side of the Iron Curtain.

The moral problem is that much of the education which we may be asked to help may seem to us uncongenial to self-government. It may be reserved for a religious or economic or political elite and so designed to perpetuate aristocracy or political dictation. We always face the questions of whether to let these factors affect our policy and whether to bargain about the way in which our educational aid is to be exploited. The principle proposed earlier for domestic education, regarding aid to schools which serve sectarian purposes, seems appropriate, even though its application on the foreign front is indeed complex. The American contribution, in money or personnel, must have its chance to advance educational aids which we support, just as in our own schools the public contribution must serve public ends. A country with a religious establishment, in which all schools are suffused with religious indoctrination, might qualify for our help only within limits set by the "child benefit" theory. We would be willing to provide materials for the education of such children as we would that of children in public secular institutions. But we would not think our money properly spent in efforts to convert or confirm the people in any particular faith.

More acute in practical terms would be the problem of our attitude toward schools frankly segregated according to creed or color. The difficulty in simply denying aid is that it does not help those denied aid, at least in respects important to us. But aid does not improve them, either. If such communities argue that the lower classes are not fit to be educated, we have no recourse except ingenious and resolute forms of pressure. Achievement of basic equality of opportunity is the objective of any American foreign aid program in education. This is not to deny the importance of the special education of experts —that "human capital" so urgently needed for economic development. But such education should not and need not be promoted so as to interfere with bringing the entire population actively into the political process. In this manner we must assert our own political morality.

PUBLIC DISCUSSION AMONG THE NATIONS

The model for international discussion was set forth in 1795 by Immanuel Kant. In *Eternal Peace*, as the great philosopher's moral idealism confronted his sad acknowledgment of men's indwelling propensity to eternal war, he outlined in crabbed but cogent statement the requirement that public policy obey the principle of "publicity." He stated the principle both negatively and positively. Policies which cannot be made public—whose success depends upon hiding from the public view—must be wrong, he said; policies which, to succeed, must be made public, must be right. Kant's premise was that men will judge policies in moral terms if the situation is made clear. The policy that works only covertly is the policy that manipulates. The policy which invites men's support as moral participants is the policy whose justice they can see.

It is such publicity which above all we need to achieve, immediately in nonmilitary ways but in the long run in military terms as well. We may decline to accept quite literally the urgent requirements which Kant formulated with respect to armies and weapons. But the old philosopher lived through many wars; he saw the absurdity in the long view for any political relations to depend upon concealment and deceit. I enter here no case for precipitate or unilateral publications of military secrets or disarmament; often such suggestions are prompted by an "intemperate morality at all costs." But the unrelenting search for matters on which we and our "enemies" can share information is an indispensable if minimal step toward real peace.

We must grant that if there are difficulties in the diffusion of public information within a nation these are multiplied many times when the discussion is with and about other nations. Yet recurring to our discussion of the schools, it is here that we find the plural principle notably benign in impact. Though the official governmental publication has the weight of national dignity behind it, by the same token it involves national commitment in ways that may prejudice free exchange. The unofficial agency—the private school or college or university—may well be more suitable for developing and conveying information which can be responsible without being official. We have tremendous opportunities to expand our education either by going abroad or by playing host to foreign students. We will not always learn from this: acquaintance with foreign cultures sometimes is hardly more than intellectual slumming—a poking around among the curious or laughable or despicable aspects of foreign peoples. But it can be a profoundly stirring adventure in discovering the dimensions of human capacity.

Such education will encounter arguments about the nature of social science—arguments familiar within our culture and some new arguments as well. To our own perplexities about how "scientific" we can be in studying society we must add the perspective of traditions in which science plays little if any part. The lesson cannot be just to "know and let know." The knowledge which the Great Community must seek to develop is a knowledge brought to bear on common political and economic and academic questions insofar as these are related to self-government. Such a knowledge cannot be in its completed form a "value-free" political science or economics or anthropology. It must, by its content and its intention, affect the people who are its subject matter. It also must clearly seek, on its factual side, a completely accurate account of how people actually behave, what they value, how they change or do not change. We must know about the others, and the others—who include the Communists—must know about us. All such knowledge has to face the difficulty that the practical considerations which inform our inquiries and our reporting are bound to be parochial. The community at which we must aim is as much to be worked out as assumed a priori.

To Americans who are convinced that our good is *the* good, or who have thrown up their hands at the notion of any good transcending national boundaries, the formulation of terms for discussion with other people must be in American categories. Like Shaw's Englishman in *Saint Joan,* such Americans insist that the angels must speak in our native tongue. Let others understand us if they can. Otherwise, we will beguile them in language which no one really believes. Such is the lonely bitterness of the man who knows himself the only good man in a naughty world.

As we seek to escape such bitterness, the clue to our efforts must be the self-government clue. It is right and proper to restrict our moral expectations for discussion to those who are self-governing or can be self-governing. The lesson is practical. It declares that common moral understanding is of one piece with that action which attends the establishment of political commitment and political machinery. This need not be a heedless march into world government. The political machinery may be local, limited, specific. But it must institute some kind of common authority which defines the terms of common understanding.

The theme, fundamentally, of our discussion with other countries must be the career and fate of self-government. This is not a new theme; it is our ancient faith; but the tumults and alarums of modern war between nations and within the individual psyche have made us forget the faith. Indeed the discussion faces obstacles more substantial than the cynical despairs of politics or psychology. There is the profound asymmetry of a discussion in which our press and other unofficial agencies are confronted by the government news bureau on the other side.

Our government, through word and deed, can conduct much of our part of the Great Discussion. A popular government will do this well and will also give our other media of expression adequate opportunity to play their part. The interplay of public and private expressions is perhaps our distinctive contribution as we contend for world opinion against the Russians and Chinese. Vigorous and persistent criticism, thoughtfully received and answered, will not prejudice our cause. This is, in fact, our principal avenue to opening up the channels of world communication for the people of the Communist world.

In the field of international negotiations we have retreated from the Kantian position expressed in Wilson's "open covenants openly arrived at." We must remember that Wilson was at pains to distinguish open covenants and the open discussion of them before negotiation from the preliminary dealings whose secrecy he took for granted. Perhaps his allowance for secrecy was excessive. But we certainly are far removed from the enthusiasm Wilson expressed in 1917 for the efforts of the new Russian government to lay before the world the secret treaties which had helped to usher in the first great war. Yet our loss of confidence in open discussion can only narrow or redirect our search for activities—in science, art, sports, health—in which fully open exchange can be brought about.

It is easier in many ways to develop common understanding with the peoples who are "not committed" and whom we hope to keep that way if not to bring to our side. Yet communication between parties unequal in power faces great difficulties too: as power difference increases, so does distrust. Our special problem is that we have assumed the mantle of British unpopularity with the colored peoples of the world in addition to the aspect of imperialism which has traditionally been our image in Latin America. In moral terms, we must overcome suspicions similar to those entertained by the young inmates of the reform school toward the keeper. We may not deserve such suspicions, but we must reckon with them.

In 1946, when the early UNESCO meetings got under way, and when efforts were made to formulate the philosophic ground for a Declaration of Human Rights, much was made of the wisdom of concentrating on specific projects in distinction from the broad principles these might embody. American spokesmen were among those who pointed to fundamental disagreements in metaphysics and political theory and who accordingly argued for focusing upon very particular undertakings. One might, they said, organize irrigation or sanitation or medical projects without deciding between Christian theology and dialectical materialism. Though the solution was prudent, the distinction is hard to maintain. Community, as the most urgent need, can be identified in general terms. Insofar as this is exemplified in specific activities—in the varied sweepings of the Augean stables of the world—we make progress. But we show little respect for our partners if we limit our part in the common effort to silently wielding the second broom or merely supplying vacuum cleaners. The full account of what is needed involves both urgent initiation of common action and patient deliberation about which stables are to be swept and what beasts, or machines, installed therein. It does scant tribute to man's talent for self-government to treat him as just a sweeper.

At the risk of putting the argument at a final disadvantage, I shall once more suggest that appeal to an absolute is useful and indeed imperative in conceiving America's part in international discussion. As we instruct our ambassador to the United Nations, we may suppose that he asks what are the fixed terms of his mission. "Well," we say, "you must be faithful to American principles." He asks then, "How faithful?" And to this we reply, "Absolutely faithful: your duty is to advance the American cause without compromise." This is not the same as America's material interest; it is rather the international order as Americans think it ought to be. In public discussion it is the American process of independent, critical, informed assertion and counterassertion. Our absolute is to serve rationality as we see it.

We should no doubt be suave in manner, relaxed and humorous, urbane, never rude or impetuous. But in stance as in action we should be utterly firm, for our own sakes and for the sake of the Great Discussion. It is the essence of the dialectic of that discussion that from the diversities of differing national views comes the most profound common clarification.

The Dialectic of International Community

For the terms of interaction of self-governing persons or groups or nations are freighted with likeness and diversity. The latter is normally where we start. Language, history, and self-interest are among its conditions; each culture begins behind its own looking glass. But such differences are not irreducible. It is only the intolerant, the man or nation who finds himself sole possessor of the truth, who blocks the common moral enterprise. The art of that enterprise is to respect the other's dignity while trying to understand him and help him understand himself. In personal relations it is as familiar as it is difficult to initiate or maintain. In relations between countries it is again familiar; yet it has been made fearfully complex as men have tangled their pursuit of decency with considerations of security and material advantage.

Freedom's problem, Spinoza said, was to find that kind of free activity which enlarges the free activity of others. The diffusion of publicity in the widest sense is the central component in such an enterprise. The many problems that beset such education of the international public are deep and vital. It is possible that such education is impossible, that a free, a self-governing world public cannot be. But a moral politics may be described as the art of the possibly impossible. Things great are, however difficult, the only ends proper to free men.

Notes to Chapters

I. The American Public and Private Interests

1. Walt Whitman, *Leaves of Grass* (Edition of 1891-92; New York: Modern Library), p. 278.
2. The letter was dated at Monticello, August 25, 1775.
3. Rousseau's Legislator or "Founding Father" was, like Rousseau himself, a proposer, not a ratifier, of basic laws. Our own Founding Fathers progressively take on the role which Rousseau defined.

II. Popular Government—The People Constituted

1. A number of phrases and ideas here are taken from Thurman Arnold's influential *The Symbols of Government* (New Haven: Yale University Press, 1935) and *The Folklore of Capitalism* (New Haven: Yale University Press, 1937).
2. Clinton Rossiter, *Conservatism in America* (New York: Alfred A. Knopf, Inc., 1955), p. 140.
3. Walter Lippmann, *Public Opinion* (New York: The MacMillan Co., 1949; first published in 1922), pp. 310 ff. Cf. also Lippmann's *The Method of Freedom* (New York: The MacMillan Co., 1934), lectures at Harvard on the Godkin Foundation.
4. It is noteworthy that, since the death of President Kennedy and the return of the "lost generation" of New Dealers to the executive branch, Democratic policies have changed little.
5. Rossiter, *Conservatism in America*, p. 263.
6. Conservatives sometimes claim "pluralism" too, but only in reference to political machineries; for them the moral basis of politics must be unitary.
7. Rossiter, *Conservatism in America*, pp. 102-03.
8. Leo Strauss, *Natural Right and History* (Chicago: University of Chicago Press, 1953).
9. John Hallowell, *The Moral Foundations of Democracy* (Chicago: University of Chicago Press, 1954).
10. Hallowell, *Moral Foundations of Democracy*, pp. 72-74.
11. Herbert J. Storing (editor), *Essays on the Scientific Study of Politics* (New York: Holt, Rinehart and Winston, 1962).

12. In Storing (ed.), *Essays*, p. 326.

13. Cf. *United States v. Schwimmer*, 279 U.S. 644 (1929), dissent of Holmes, A. J.; and *Cantwell v. Connecticut*, 310 U.S. 296 (1940).

14. Morton White, *Social Thought in America: The Revolt against Formalism* (Boston: Beacon Press, 1957).

15. *Abrams v. United States*, 250 U.S. 616 (1919).

16. Rossiter, *Conservatism in America*, p. 110.

17. Samuel A. Stouffer, *Communism, Conformity and Civil Liberties* (New York: Doubleday & Co., 1955), p. 186.

18. William O. Douglas, A. J., in *Zorach v. Clauson*, 343 U.S. 306 (1952).

19. *Ballard v. United States*, 322 U.S. 78 (1944).

20. This is intended to convey the meaning defined by G. E. Moore in *Principia Ethica*.

21. The "empiricists" take widely differing attitudes toward the role of normative judgments in political inquiry. Steffens became finally an earnest Marxist; on the other hand, Jane Addams combined a passion for facts with a pervasive devotion to ideals which might guide both theory and practice.

22. As noted above, the same allegiance is professed by conservatives. The popularity of Federalist Paper Ten with both sceptics and conservatives suggests that it may also be congenial to the middle path followed here.

23. Arthur M. Schlesinger, *Paths to the Present* (New York: The MacMillan Co., 1939), Chapter II.

24. See Storing (ed.), *Essays*.

25. David B. Truman, *The Governmental Process: Political Interests and Public Opinion* (New York: Alfred A. Knopf, Inc., 1952).

26. *Ibid.*, p. 535.

27. *Loc. cit.*

28. *Loc. cit.*

29. Cf. Truman's account of the A.M.A. and many labor unions. Truman notes that all such groups show some deference to the "democratic mold."

30. Truman, *Governmental Process*, p. 102.

31. *Ibid.*, p. 129.

32. *Ibid.*, p. 131.

33. *United States v. Rumely*, 345 U.S. 41 (1953).

34. *Hannah v. Larche*, 363 U.S. 420 (1960).

35. Walter Lippmann, *The Good Society* (Boston: Little, Brown & Co., 1937), p. 93. Selections from *The Good Society*, Copyright 1936, 1937, 1943 by Walter Lippmann, are reprinted by permission of Little, Brown and Company, publishers.

36. *Ibid.*, p. 346.

37. *Ibid.*, pp. 346 and 347; here we have the essence of the "public philosophy" of 1955.

38. *Ibid.*, p. 347.
39. *Ibid.*, pp. 272-73.
40. *Ibid.*, p. 366.
41. *Ibid.*, p. 348.

III. ACTIVE GOVERNMENT—THE PEOPLE'S BUSINESS
AND THE PEOPLE'S SCHOOLS

1. Lippmann, in *Public Opinion*, p. 289, offered a notable criticism of congressional investigations, describing them as "legalized atrocities" which do not stop "at cannibalism."

2. Legally this has meant appeal to the Fifth Amendment property freedom rather than the First Amendment freedom of thought. The latter has been more frequently invoked in recent years.

3. The lines are from Edward Thomas' description of Brooke at the time of his graduation from the university.

4. The government involved here may be national, state, or local; but in the last analysis the national government must see that coherence of effort is assured.

5. Most of our educational establishment, though supported by taxes, is locally governed and has no express responsibility to the national public. In this sense it is effectively "private."

6. *Lochner v. New York*, 198 U.S. 45 (1905).

7. *Tyson & Bros. v. Banton*, 273 U.S. 418 (1927).

8. *Adkins v. Children's Hospital*, 261 U.S. 525 (1923).

9. *Jones & Laughlin Steel Corporation v. National Labor Relations Board*, 301 U.S. 1 (1937).

10. Mr. Justice Holmes is fairly associated, with due allowance for his special intellectual bent, with the Darwinian identification of virtue and power. It is plausible to suggest that Holmes would favor a public strengthening of the weak rather than a policy to weaken the strong. Public action, through education or material aid, to fit competitors for the struggle is in principle better than reducing the potential of others. Of course, such policies intensify the pressures exerted upon the government.

11. Lippmann, *Public Opinion*, Part VIII.

12. *Ibid.*, pp. 402-05.

13. In Section VI, "Conclusions," of *General Interim Report of the House Select Committee on Lobbying Activities*, 81st Congress, 2d Session, 1950.

14. *Minersville School Board v. Gobitis*, 310 U.S. 586 (1940).

15. *West Virginia Board of Education v. Barnette*, 319 U.S. 624 (1943).

16. *Everson v. Board of Education*, 330 U.S. 1 (1947).

17. *McCollum v. Board of Education*, 333 U.S. 203 (1948), and *Zorach v. Clauson*, 343 U.S. 306 (1952).

18. *Engel v. Vitale*, 370 U.S. 421 (1962).

19. *School District of Abington Township, Pa., et al. v. Edward Lewis Schempp,* 83 Sup. Ct. 1560 (1963).

20. *Adler v. Board of Education,* 342 U.S. 485 (1952).

21. *Pierce v. Society of Sisters,* 268 U.S. 510 (1925).

22. *Engel v. Vitale;* the Court's outlawry of Bible reading in public schools a year later evoked far less overt protest (in *Abington Township v. Schempp*). But local practices have been slow to follow the Court's ruling.

23. Letter from Madison to Jefferson, January 22, 1786, in Irving Brant, *James Madison: The Nationalist* (New York: Bobbs-Merrill, 1948), p. 354.

IV. RESPONSIBLE GOVERNMENT—THE FREEDOM OF PUBLIC DISCUSSION

1. In A. W. Peach (ed.), *Selections from the Works of Thomas Paine* (New York: Harcourt, Brace & Co., 1928), p. 4.

2. Lippmann, *The Public Philosophy* (Boston: Little, Brown & Co., 1955), p. 66. Lippmann, like Paine, sets government over against society: government must, Lippmann says, act continually against popular impulse, though still on behalf of the people's deeper or "better" nature. Cf. pp. 41-42.

3. Theodore White, *The Making of the President, 1960* (New York: Pocket Books, Inc., 1961), p. 10.

4. White, *op. cit.,* pp. 361-62, links this conception with the philosophy of the Democratic Party. Liberal Republicans, in fact, seem to take substantially the same view.

5. White observes that Walter Lippmann predicts a ready reaction by government in the event of an abuse of press service rights (*op. cit.,* p. 336).

6. We have here once more an illustration of both negative and positive elements in freedom, of the absence of restraint and the power to act effectively. A man has freedom of speech as he is both unchecked in expression and also able to reach a genuinely attentive audience. The Constitutional freedom of speech is the public status of being heard on topics of public concern, as the freedom of voting is both being unrestrained and also having one's vote counted. "In America," White remarks, "all the people help choose" (*op. cit.,* p. 211); and so far they may be said to enjoy the freedom of public speech.

7. *Thornhill v. Alabama,* 310 U.S. 88 (1940).

8. *Senn v. Tile Layers Protective Union,* 301 U.S. 478 (1937): "Members of a union might, without special statutory authorization by a State, make known the facts of a labor dispute, for freedom of speech is guaranteed by the Federal Constitution."

9. A footnote at the beginning of Chapter II of *On Liberty* restricts intereference by government to cases of direct instigation to crime.

10. "True Conservatives," according to Rossiter, hold no laws absolute.

11. *Dennis et al. v. United States*, 341 U.S. 494 (1951).

12. Fourth paragraph from end of Chapter I of *On Liberty*.

13. *Sweezy v. New Hampshire*, 354 U.S. 234 (1957).

14. *Zorach v. Clauson*, 343 U.S. 306 (1952).

15. *The New York Times*, Sunday, Sept. 25, 1962, p. 50.

16. In cases preceding this declaration, espousal of the "preferred position" of freedom of speech had "approached" the absolutist position.

17. Hugo Black, A. J., James Madison Lecture of 1961, 35 *New York University Law Review* 882.

18. *The New York Times Co. v. Sullivan*, 376 U.S. 254 (1963).

19. Thus C. H. Pritchett, *Civil Liberties and the Vinson Court* (Chicago: University of Chicago Press, 1954), p. 79.

20. In *Freedom of Speech* (New York: Harcourt, Brace & Howe, 1920) at p. 16, Zechariah Chafee suggested, despite his devotion to Mr. Justice Holmes, that true and sober criticism of fire exit facilities could hardly be restricted. It is not easy to say exactly what is "true" or "sober"—the manner of statement and temper of the audience are crucial. As Mill put it, words lose their immunity when they take on the quality of actions.

21. Lippmann, *The Public Philosophy*, pp. 47-57.

22. Thomas Reed Powell, revered leader among New Deal legal philosophers, when challenged as to his loyalty to the Constitution used to say, "Of course I support the Constitution; it has supported me in my teaching at Harvard these many years." As so often, the humor is appropriately tinctured with interplay of public and private overtones.

23. *Chaplinsky v. New Hampshire*, 315 U.S. 568 (1942).

24. *Lochner v. New York*, 198 U.S. 45 (1905); quotations are from the last paragraph of Holmes' dissent.

25. *Beauharnais v. Illinois*, 343 U.S. 250 (1952).

26. Lippmann, *The Public Philosophy*, p. 132.

27. *Loc. cit.*

28. Cf. Mr. Justice Frankfurter's dissent in *West Virginia v. Barnette*, 319 U.S. 624 (1943).

29. "Subversion" and "sedition" are terms which blur the distinction between thoughts and actions; they should be dropped from usage. At present they mean in effect "spreading bad thoughts."

30. *American Communications Association v. Douds*, 339 U.S. 382 (1950).

31. *Yates v. United States*, 354 U.S. 298 (1957).

32. As Arthur M. Schlesinger, Jr., put the criterion in *The Vital Center* (Boston: Houghton Mifflin Co., 1949), "we must tolerate dangerous opinions. . . . But we must draw the line at the opinion which results in the immediate and violent obliteration of the conditions of subsequent discussion." (P. 199)

33. *Schenck v. United States*, 249 U.S. 47 (1919).

34. In the Second Circuit Court of Appeals: *United States v. Dennis et al.,* 183 Fed.2d at 212 (1950).

35. *Palko v. Connecticut,* 302 U.S. 319 (1937).

36. *United States v. Carolene Products,* 304 U.S. 104 (1939).

37. *Whitney v. California,* 274 U.S. 357 (1927).

38. In 35 *New York University Law Review,* pp. 874-75.

39. These cases include *Barenblatt v. United States,* 360 U.S. 109 (1959); *Braden v. United States,* 365 U.S. 431 (1961); and *Wilkinson v. United States,* 365 U.S. 399 (1961).

40. *United States v. Ballard,* 322 U.S. 78 (1944).

41. *Davis v. Beason,* 133 U.S. 333 (1890).

42. *Masses Publishing Co. v. Patten,* 244 Fed. 535 (S.D.N.Y. 1917).

43. *United States v. Dennis et al.,* 183 F.2d 201 (1950).

44. *The Spirit of Liberty: Papers and Addresses of Learned Hand,* ed. Irving Dilliard (New York: Alfred A. Knopf, Inc., 1952), pp. 99-100.

V. American Freedom and the Wider World

1. Such materials include Ray Stannard Baker's *Life and Letters,* which are pro-Wilson but not uncritical, the biographical volumes by Arthur Link, Herbert Hoover and others, Allen Nevins' life of Henry White, and Wilson's own *Public Papers.*

2. George F. Kennan, *American Diplomacy 1900-1950* (New York: New American Library of World Literature, 1952).

3. In fact, Kennan seems to level his attack primarily upon the policies of John Foster Dulles.

4. See *American Diplomacy 1900-1950,* Chapters VII and VIII.

5. "The Mainsprings of American Foreign Policy: The National Interest v. Moral Abstractions," *American Political Science Review,* XVIV, No. 4, pp. 853-54.

6. Many phrases and arguments here are taken from Kant's *Eternal Peace.*

Index of Names and Cases

Abrams v. U.S., 39
Adams, John, 40
Adkins v. Children's Hospital, 75
Adler v. Board of Education, 90
American Communications Association v. Douds, 121
Aristotle, 31, 58
Arnold, Thurman, 27, 60

Bailey, Stephen K., 67
Ballard v. U.S., 19, 128
Barenblatt v. U.S., 127
Beauharnais v. Illinois, 117
Bentley, Arthur F., 46, 48
Berns, Walter, 34, 36, 118, 119, 120
Black, Hugo, 56, 91, 109, 124
Braden v. U.S., 127
Brandeis, Louis D., 106, 124
Brooke, Rupert, 70
Brown, John, 2

Calhoun, John C., 40
Cantwell v. Conn., 37
Cardozo, Benjamin, 124
Carnegie, Andrew, 87
Chaplinsky v. N.H., 116
Clark, Thomas, 109
Cleon, 6
Coke, Edward, 62

Davis v. Beason, 128
Dennis et al. v. U.S., 108, 109, 110, 116, 117, 119, 121-23
de Tocqueville, Alexis. *See* Tocqueville, Alexis de

Dewey, John, 13-16, 20, 21, 27, 51, 69, 99, 100
Douglas, William O., 56, 91, 109, 111

Emerson, Ralph Waldo, 2
Engel v. Vitale, 86, 93, 94
Everson v. N.J., 86, 93

Frankfurter, Felix, 85, 109, 116, 121
Freud, Sigmund, 13

Galbraith, John K., 79
Galilei, Galileo, 62, 63

Hallowell, John H., 28, 31, 32, 34, 37, 38, 42
Hamilton, Alexander, 25
Hand, Learned, 123, 128-30
Hannah v. Larche, 55-57
Hegel, Georg W. F., 15
Hitler, Adolf, 120
Hobbes, Thomas, 31
Holmes, Oliver W., Jr., 39, 74-75, 78, 79, 116, 122, 123, 129
Hughes, Charles E., 79
Hume, David, 11, 21

Jackson, Robert H., 117
James, William, 129
Jefferson, Thomas, 4-7, 9, 11, 41, 66, 93
Jesus, 107
Jones & Laughlin v. NLRB, 79

Kant, Immanuel, 9, 10, 11, 37, 39, 119, 139, 148-49, 151
Kelly, Walt, 23
Kennan, George F., 134-35
Kennedy, John F., 3
Kirk, Russell, 28

LaFollette, Robert M., 133
Leibniz, Gottfried W., 11
Lenin, V. I., 79, 120
Lippmann, Walter, 25, 59-63 *passim*, 77, 80, 102, 112, 119, 120
Lipset, Seymour, 44
Lochner v. N.Y., 74, 116
Locke, John, 31, 65
Lubell, Samuel, 26
Lynd, Robert S. and Helen M., 68

McCollum v. Board of Education, 86, 94
McReynolds, James C., 94
Madison, James, 4, 11, 24, 45, 94
Marx, Karl, 79, 89
Masses v. Patten, 129
Mill, John Stuart, 2, 3, 15, 22, 37, 89, 96, 107-08, 115, 122, 138
Minersville School Board v. Gobitis, 85, 121
Minton, Sherman, 90
Morgenthau, Hans J., 135-38
Murphy, Frank, 106

New York Times Co. v. Sullivan, 109

Paine, Thomas, 101-02, 112
Palko v. Conn., 124
Pierce v. Society of Sisters, 93, 94
Plato, 21, 41, 51, 58, 61, 84, 96, 110

Randolph, John, 5, 6
Rockwell, George L., 116, 117
Roosevelt, Franklin D., 25
Roosevelt, Theodore, 133

Rossiter, Clinton, 23, 28, 30, 31
Rousseau, Jean-Jacques, 9, 10, 13, 19, 24, 62, 78, 103, 108, 141

Schenck v. U.S., 122, 123
Schlesinger, Arthur M., 45
School District of Abington v. Schempp, 86, 94
Senn v. Tile Layers Protective Union, 106
Shaw, George Bernard, 150
Smith, Adam, 78, 145
Socrates, 6, 10, 13, 67, 107, 115, 124, 146
Sophists, 10, 82, 88, 113, 115
Spencer, Herbert, 74
Steffens, Lincoln, 44
Stewart, Potter, 93
Stone, Harlan F., 124
Stouffer, Samuel A., 41
Strauss, Leo, 28, 31, 34, 35, 42, 46, 118
Stuart, James I of England, 62
Sweezy v. N.H., 109

Terminiello, Arthur (*Terminiello v. Chicago*), 118
Themistocles, 84
Thoreau, Henry David, 2, 125, 126
Thornhill v. Alabama, 106
Tocqueville, Alexis de, 24, 40
Truman, David B., 46-50, 53, 54
Tyson & Bros. v. Banton, 74

U.S. v. Carolene Products, 124
U.S. v. Dennis et al. (183 Fed. 2d at 212), 123, 129
U.S. v. Rumely, 55-57
U.S. v. Schwimmer, 37

Vinson, Fred M., 108, 109, 110, 123

Weinstein, Leo, 46-47
West Virginia Board of Education v. Barnette, 86, 121
White, Morton, 38

White, Theodore, 102
Whitman, Walt, 1
Whitney v. California, 124
Wilkinson v. U.S., 127
Wilson, Woodrow, 12, 25, 26, 87,
  132-34, 135, 151, 152

Winthrop, John, 31, 33

Yates v. U.S., 122

Zorach v. Clauson, 42, 86, 109, 111